T0003839

LIVING THROUGH THE
INDUSTRIAL REVOLUTION

INDUSTRIAL REVOLUTION

LIVING THROUGH THE
INDUSTRIAL REVOLUTION

STELLA DAVIES

Routledge
Taylor & Francis Group

LONDON AND NEW YORK

First published in 1966

•••••••••••2006 by
Routledge
2 Park Square, Milton Park, Abingdon, Oxfordshire OX14 4RN
711 Third Avenue, New York, NY 10017

First issued in paperback 2014

Routledge is an imprint of the Taylor and Francis Group, an informa business

© 1966 Stella Davies

The publishers have made every effort to contact authors and copyright holders of the works reprinted in the *Economic History* series. This has not been possible in every case, however, and we would welcome correspondence from those individuals or organisations we have been unable to trace.

These reprints are taken from original copies of each book. In many cases the condition of these originals is not perfect. The publisher has gone to great lengths to ensure the quality of these reprints, but wishes to point out that certain characteristics of the original copies will, of necessity, be apparent in reprints thereof.

British Library Cataloguing in Publication Data
A CIP catalogue record for this book
is available from the British Library

Living through the Industrial Revolution
ISBN 0-415-37840-0 (volume)
ISBN 0-415-37837-0 (subset)
ISBN 0-415-28619-0 (set)

ISBN13: 978-1-138-86478-8 (pbk)
ISBN13: 978-0-415-37840-6 (hbk)

Routledge Library Editions: Economic History

LIVING THROUGH THE
INDUSTRIAL REVOLUTION

By the same Author

NORTH COUNTRY BRED: A WORKING-CLASS
FAMILY CHRONICLE

EXPLORING THE WORLD

LIVING THROUGH THE INDUSTRIAL REVOLUTION

by

STELLA DAVIES

PH.D., M.A.

Routledge & Kegan Paul

LONDON

First published 1966
by Routledge & Kegan Paul Limited
Broadway House, 68–74 Carter Lane
London, E.C.4

IN MEMORY OF MY HUSBAND
W. O. DAVIES

Contents

Illustrations

Preface

IN this book I have tried to tell the story of the Industrial Revolution through the lives of those who lived through it and made it possible. People from many walks of life appear in its pages—the great landowners and country gentlemen, farmers and farm labourers, millowners and mill workers, miners, steel smelters, women and children machine minders and many others. Although I have been mainly concerned with the new industrial inventions, I have also sketched in many areas of social life which were little affected by the great changes which were taking place between the years 1760–1830. These changes have affected our present society and my intention has been to recount our debt to the past and to link it with the present.

Views about the Industrial Revolution differ widely; it has been and continues to be the subject of much debate. We, are, perhaps, too near it in time to be able to view it objectively. The books written about it fill many library shelves. I am indebted to many writers for factual material. For the expression of ideas and attitudes, other than my own, I have gone to those who lived in the period. They, or some of them, wrote diaries and letters, gave evidence before the various commissions of inquiry or, by their actions, made clear how they felt about the new society which was in the making. I hope that I have dealt justly with them whether I agree with them or not.

As this book is not a textbook for scholars but, rather, for general reading, the pages are unencumbered by footnote references. There are plenty of books that will provide these for the reader who wishes to go further than I have done. Any librarian will welcome and help a serious inquirer. The extracts in the appendices give some idea of the kind of sources that I have used.

As in all my writing I have been encouraged and aided by Mrs. O'Brien and Miss Olive Hitchcock who have helped with the index, corrected mistakes and syntax and have sometimes been allowed to curb my informalities of style and expression.

I

Making, Buying and Selling

For most people who earn their living, the working day begins with the sound of an alarm clock, a hurried breakfast and a journey. By train, bus, car, bicycle or on foot vast throngs of people make their way to factories, shops or offices, where they work in association with others to produce, distribute or sell the goods which society requires. This is so usual that we take it for granted but it was not always so. That these conditions exist today is the consequence of certain changes which took place during the eighteenth and nineteenth centuries. Perhaps the greatest change was the use of power to drive machines, for this meant that a mounting volume of goods became available instead of the thin trickle previously made by hand. Moreover, the use of power-driven machines made far-reaching changes in ways of living.

Other changes in production took place. In agriculture, mining, iron and steel making, textiles, machines were introduced and improved; transport was made quicker and easier; new methods of organization were evolved. There is no precise date for these advances but in the years between 1760–1830 change was so rapid that the period became known as that of the Industrial Revolution. It is not a happy description, for revolutions suggest an over-throw or destruction of the past and a starting again on entirely new lines. This was far from being so during the industrial revolution. Many changes had taken place over previous centuries which led up to it and made it possible. After 1830 methods of produc-tion continued to evolve and there were profound alterations in society, many of them the direct result of the industrial revolution or of the need to deal with the problems of which it was the cause. So, in order to understand what happened in those fateful seventy years which have influenced our lives to the extent that we live in their aftermath, it is necessary to look both forwards and backwards from them. Let us first look backwards.

In small and simple societies, most of the things that are needed are made on the spot, using materials that are to hand or which can easily be transported. There is little division of labour except between men and women for nearly everybody can make the articles which are in common use. For example, the making of furs into clothing was the job of all Eskimo women, there was no special dressmaker or tailor; hunting reindeer or walrus was the job of all the men. Nevertheless, even in primitive societies, tools and weapons came to be made by specialists who became

2

skilled by concentrating on a particular job. When men learned how to mine and fashion gold, tin, copper and iron, specialization was essential, for the processes of manufacturing metals are long and intricate and the ores which contain them are not found everywhere. They have to be sought and transported. This can best be done if the metal-workers are not concerned with growing their own food. A further division of labour followed: farmers grew food and exchanged some of it for the products of the metal-workers' craft. Other specializations arose: pot-making, wood- and leather-working, for example. Because the work was done with simple tools and equipment, the craftsman could work alone or in a small group and did not need elaborate premises. For many hundreds of years, clothes, furniture, tools, weapons and most of the things in use were made by craftsmen and their apprentices in workshops attached to their homes or in the home itself.

Most craftsmen lived in towns or in large villages where there was a market. Their customers came to them, ordered a chair, a pair of boots or a length of cloth. The craftsman bought the material required, made the commodity and was paid by the customer. Craftsmen organized themselves in guilds according to their craft in order to strengthen their bargaining power over merchant and customer, to maintain the standard of their work and also to help each other in times of distress. In the late Middle Ages the guild system and with it the craftsman–customer relationship began to be superseded and today it has almost disappeared in England. It can still be found over much of Asia and Africa and also in eastern Europe. Near the Acropolis in Athens, surrounded by blocks of modern flats, there are streets where tailors, shoemakers, smiths and carpenters make their goods by hand and to order at the back of open-fronted shops, much as was done when the Acropolis was built over two thousand years ago.

Luxury goods, such as silk, high quality woollen cloth, dried fruits, sugar and spices were brought into England by foreign merchants and were sold at fairs which, as distinct from markets, were not held weekly but only on special occasions. In Shakespeare's play, *The Winter's Tale*, one of the characters on his way to a fair says to himself, 'What am I to buy for our sheepshearing feast? Three pounds of sugar, five pounds of currants, rice—what will this sister of mine do with rice? . . . I must have saffron to colour the pies; mace, nutmegs, seven, a race or two of ginger, four pounds of prunes.'

Home-produced goods which were only needed from time to time, such as pots, pans, horses and cattle, were sold at fairs; week-to-week requirements were bought in the local market unless they were purchased directly from the producer. Except in London and a few other large towns there were no retail shops as we understand the term. Many country towns still hold markets, often in the centre of the town. Before the advent of the motor car, the main

4

thoroughfare was a good place for people to congregate. It is often called 'Market Street', even if the market is no longer held there.

Towards the end of the Middle Ages and increasingly afterwards, many goods which had been previously imported were made in England. The most important of these was woollen cloth which the English weavers had learned to make to a high quality and in great variety. Large areas of land which had hitherto been forest, heath or moorland, frequented by deer, were turned into pasture for sheep in order to increase the supply of wool. Rather than being allowed to wander over a large area, sheep do better and pasture is improved if the sheep are restricted to a limited area until the herbage is eaten and then moved to another place where the process is repeated. Also, when managed in this way, they are easier to control. Forest, heath and moorland were divided into fields by walls built with the stones which lay on the surface. This was the origin of the stone walls which climb up the hills of the Pennines, Dartmoor, the Cotswolds, the Lake district and other parts of England where rock and sheep are present.

In the sixteenth century, the enclosed fields did not reach much higher than the flanks of the hills but, as the demand for wool increased, the walls were built higher and higher, leaving less and less room for the deer. Hunting deer for food and sport, which had been very popular in the Middle Ages, was no longer easy or enjoyable; it fell out of fashion and the diminished herds were placed in deer parks where their descendants can still sometimes be seen. The enclosure of land for rearing sheep and the parkland of the Tudor gentry were the beginning of a new type of landscape in the English countryside.

Most people know that the Chancellor of England sits, in the House of Lords, on a woolsack as an acknowledgment of the value of wool to England during the Middle Ages. The making of woollen cloth was even more profitable because the value of the labour involved in making an article increases its value over that of the raw material. When London Bridge was rebuilt in the sixteenth century, the piers of the bridge were founded on woolsacks. They made a firm yet elastic base and they were also regarded as a symbol of the importance of wool to the port of London. England benefited greatly by the trade in woollen cloth and many people grew rich as a consequence. The comfortless medieval house with little privacy, hardly any furniture and a fire in the middle of the one large room fell into disuse. Tudor halls with glass windows, oak panelling, ornamental fireplaces set in chimneys, joined tables instead of trestles and four-poster feather beds were built for sheep farmers and cloth merchants. The great landlords no longer lived in grim stone castles but in mansions set about with gardens and orchards.

The function of the merchant developed and altered during the Tudor period. In addition to importing goods from abroad, he had always been concerned

6

with getting the goods to the customer by buying them from the producer and arranging for their transport. This side of his work grew as more home-produced goods became available. Although many producers of woollen cloth took their 'piece' to the local market and sold it themselves, others lived in districts remote from centres of population so more cloth was made than could be absorbed locally. The bulk of cloth made by one weaver was small; a merchant was needed to collect a sufficient number of pieces to make transport to London an economic proposition. In London, the demand was greater and cloth could be shipped abroad.

The need for a merchant was particularly great in areas like the Pennine country which had been very thinly populated before the sixteenth century. With the introduction of cloth-making, the north of England began to fill up but the pattern of settlement was different from that made in earlier times. In the Middle Ages, most people lived either in towns or in villages as they do now though, by modern standards, both towns and villages were very small. The isolated dwelling or tiny hamlet was exceptional. From the sixteenth century onward, farm-houses and hamlets of half a dozen or so cottages were built on the heaths, on the edges of the mosses, in clearings in the woodlands and on the slopes of the hills.

Wool from the sheep on the newly enclosed pastures about the isolated settlements was spun and woven in the farm-houses and cottages. Farming in the north was mainly concerned with cattle and sheep, for climate and soil made corn-growing difficult. In arable country, threshing corn with a flail by hand kept farm-workers busy in the winter. Cattle and sheep needed little attention for all but the breeding stock were slaughtered and salted in November. A home industry provided work in winter and the money earned paid the rent.

The demand for wool soon outstripped the local supply, even for the weavers on the farms and more so for the cottagers who had little or no land. Merchants responded to local shortages by buying wool in other districts and selling it to the weavers. By the seventeenth century they were bringing wool into the Pennine country from Wales, Ireland, the Lake district and from the Cheviot hills on the borders of Scotland. Finished cloth needs many more processes than spinning and weaving. Merchants arranged for the transport of unfinished cloth from the weaver to the fuller, the dyer and the shearers, who cut the surface to produce a nap. Cloth often travelled a considerable distance and passed through a number of hands.

A London merchant would come to Lancashire 'to provide and bespeak the making of the cloths he wanted, employing an agent to receive the cloth so ordered, get it fulled at Middleton, dressed by the shearmen at Manchester and Salford' and forward it to London. The agent bought the cloth in the hamlets and villages in the country to the north of Manchester. This complicated organization of the cloth trade was reported in the seventeenth century. It was based on small groups of people working in their homes as in earlier times but now these units of production were scattered over the countryside. The producers depended increasingly on merchants for their supply of raw material and for the disposal of the goods they made.

Merchants were called by various names, all meaning much the same thing: middlemen, traders, clothiers, chapmen, factors, tackmen. The term 'merchant' was commonly used to describe those in a large way of business; the other terms were used for the smaller men who worked on their own account or as go-betweens for the large merchants and small producers. This method of making and selling goods is called the 'Domestic System'. The scattered groups of workers used tools or simple machines which were operated by hand or foot. Quantities of goods were made and marketed in this way between the reign of Queen Elizabeth I and the end of the eighteenth century. The domestic system was adopted not only for cloth-making but for many other commodities and in some instances it lasted into modern times.

The history of the Mosley family shows clearly how the system worked in relation to the merchants. The Mosleys were originally tenant farmers in Withington, a village about five miles from Manchester, which, in the sixteenth century, was also a village though a large one. The Mosleys had some arable

9

land and, near to their farm, there was a large stretch of uncultivated grassland called Barlow Moor and here the villagers pastured their sheep and cattle. The first Mosley of whom there is any record was called Jenkyn and, in 1465, he married a wife who brought £50 to the marriage as a dowry, at that time quite a substantial sum for a farmer. Jenkyn had several sons; some of them continued to farm; three of the younger ones became merchants, travelling the countryside round Manchester, buying cloth from the weavers.

A grandson, Oswald, built a house with a warehouse on the banks of the Medlock, now a murky stream but then pleasant enough to have a garden and orchard running down to it. His brother, Nicholas, organized the collection of the cloth and Oswald arranged for its transport to London where another brother saw to its sale. In 1567, when Nicholas was about forty years of age, the London brother died, so Nicholas went to London and took over the selling side of the business, leaving Oswald to run the buying side from Manchester. The Mosleys prospered. Oswald became an important local figure and held many offices in connection with local administration. He was, at one time or another, overseer of the fountains which supplied Manchester with water, tax collector, supervisor of the cleansing of the ditch which ran through the town and Reeve, that is, representative of the people at the Lord of the Manor's court.

Nicholas had a stand in Blackwell Hall, the great cloth market in London. Towards the end of his life

10

he was made Lord Mayor of London. Many merchants attained this honour from lowly beginnings, thus giving rise to the legend of Dick Whittington. Nicholas went back to Manchester for his last years. He purchased the manors of Manchester and Withington. He built, on the outskirts of Withington, a handsome stone hall with mullion windows, an ornamented roof, gardens and an orchard. Here he died at the age of 85. While his body was being prepared for burial, £400 in gold was found in his feather bed. He had a large family and provided well for them, leaving his eldest son £1,000 a year and to the others proportionately.

Oswald also lived to a great age. He moved from the house on the bank of the Medlock to a large hall which he built in Ancoats, then a pleasant country district, now a slum. An interesting pair of brasses in Manchester Cathedral commemorate Oswald and his wife and family. One shows Oswald and his wife, his five sons and three daughters; the other shows Oswald's eldest son, also named Oswald, *his* wife and also five sons and three daughters. In their lives, Nicholas and Oswald almost spanned the sixteenth century. During this time Manchester, from being an obscure agricultural village, developed rapidly into an important centre of industry.

Not all merchants did as well or operated on as large a scale as the Mosleys. With goods and money passing through so many hands many middlemen had difficulty in collecting debts and so fell into debt themselves. Richard Heywood, of Little Lever, was the son of a carpenter who also had a farm which supplied most of their food. Richard and his father, as well as attending to the farm and carpentering, also wove fustian, a cheap coarse cloth made of a mixture of wool and linen. Their work did not lack variety. Richard married when he was 19 years old and set up as a trader. Soon, he was heavily in debt and had to 'skulk in holes and flee'. For a year he and his wife lived in hiding for fear of his creditors, who had obtained a summons against him for his arrest. Richard was helped by his father and 'many other friends whom he raised up beyond expectation' and after a while he was able to pay some of his debts and start trading for a London merchant. All went well for a time. Richard completed the payment of the money he owed, educated two of his sons for the Church and gave his four daughters £60 each as a dowry. He bought a house and some land and invested some of his money in 'colepits', small coal-mining ventures which were just beginning in Lancashire and Cheshire.

When he was nearing 60 years of age, his London merchant began to get behind with the payments for the cloth sent to him by Richard. Again Richard found himself in serious difficulties. His son, Oliver, from whose diaries this account is taken, wrote, 'This, together with his son's prodigality, his own old age and forgetfulness but chiefly by the hand of God, he was cast into debt of £1,200; but by the blessing of

God and the pains of some relations he got wrestled through and paid to the full the most considerable debts and sold most of his land.'

The affairs of a Rochdale middleman were even more unfortunate. In this instance three people were concerned: a London merchant called Bernard Emott, a Manchester agent and a Rochdale factor. The factor collected the pieces of cloth from the weavers, the agent arranged for the pieces to be finished and the London merchant exported them. The Rochdale factor died and his widow tried to carry on the business. In 1647, she contracted through the agent to supply Emott with five packs of cloth, each pack to contain seven pieces, at £23 15s. a pack. The cloth was delivered by instalments but the widow was unable to obtain the money from Emott. The widow pled that 'she, but a woman and living distant from there, should be at great stress to get her money, she not being able to travel to London'. She already had £120 'laid forth' in payment to the weavers. She employed a lawyer to bring pressure on Emott but he does not seem to have been successful for four years later the widow was still unpaid.

The difficulty in getting their money, experienced by Richard Heywood and the Rochdale widow was often repeated but, in general, the majority of people must have honoured their obligations or the credit system would have broken down. Society cannot hold together unless most of its members keep the rules. Sometimes, in credit transactions, a pledge

13

would be demanded, such as a silver cup or a gold ring or a mortgage might be taken on house or land. When the weaver's reputation for honesty was well established, the factor would deliver the wool 'on trust to the buyer without speciality or witness and only enter the same in their books'.

An amusing example of belated honesty is shown in the following quotation from the will of a farmer-weaver: 'To the woolman in respect that I bought a pack of wool from him which, when I weighed it, I found was more by a stone than I bought.' The weaver had not been able to bring himself to tell the wool dealer of the mistake, though evidently it weighed on his conscience. Nevertheless, as restitution was only to be made after his death, it would be his heir and not he who would foot the bill.

Experience in making goods for the market and in buying and selling grew steadily until, by the eighteenth century, there were large numbers of people who earned their living, or part of it, in this manner. The way was eased and a springboard was provided for the immense expansion of trade and industry which resulted from the industrial revolution. Over large areas of the English countryside the population was no longer engaged only in agriculture. They were making many different kinds of things to sell and were accustomed to this way of life.

2

The Domestic Industries

W H E N, in addition to wool and linen, cotton and silk became available for making textiles, the organization of the supply of raw material became more intricate for cotton and silk were imported from distant countries. The new materials required ocean-sailing ships for their transport, ports and docks, agents in foreign countries and elaborate methods of payment both for the raw material and the finished goods. Never before had such large quantities of raw material been imported for manufacture in this country and never before had British exports been so valuable. This set the pattern for our present society which is largely dependent on materials brought from abroad.

At first, the making of silk was in the hands of Huguenot refugees from France who came to this country to escape religious and political persecution. They kept their craft a closely guarded secret. Silk in cocoons does not need spinning for this has been done by the silkworm. To produce a thread for weaving, it is necessary to unwind and twist the filament; this process is called 'throwing'. Throwing and weaving silk entails a certain amount of waste and, during the seventeenth century, English merchants purchased this waste from the Huguenots and distributed it about the country for the making of buttons. Thus a new domestic industry was started and the new textile came into English hands.

Fastening clothes with buttons began towards the end of the sixteenth century; before that time, clothes were held together by brooches or clasped by belts or the openings were laced by 'points' (thongs with firm ends). The transition from points to buttons can be noticed in two references, one from *Twelfth Night* and the other from *King Lear*. In *Twelfth Night* the clown is sparring with Maria, 'Not so, neither; but I am resolved on two points.' Maria then makes a pun, using the other sense of the term, 'If one break, the other will hold; or if both break, your gaskins fall.' In *Lear* at a moment of unbearable anguish, the King, mourning Cordelia's death, feels that he is choking. He struggles with his cloak and appeals to Albany, 'Pray you undo this button.'

The making of buttons was done by women and children, using a needle. The buttons were very elaborate; men's coats of the seventeenth and eighteenth centuries often had two or three dozens of them on fronts and sleeves. It was reported that 'an active woman, working diligently, could earn four shillings a week' for making them. Children of six years and over could and did assist in preparing the thread. The wives and children of thousands of farm-labourers engaged in this work. No expensive tool was needed and, in the eighteenth century when the labourer's wage was round about six shillings a week, the additional four shillings to the family income would mean a great deal.

Waste from the silk looms was also made into stockings, garters, fringes and sewing-silk. Other uses were found for it and all these by-products found work for English people for the Huguenots were fully occupied in the more skilled weaving and throwing; they did not consider working on silk waste worth their while. England was growing much wealthier during the eighteenth century and more people had money to spend on silk coats, knee-breeches and dresses. Gradually the Huguenots relinquished the throwing process and concentrated on weaving. Merchants purchased the raw silk and distributed it to English domestic workers in London and later to places farther north. In course of time the throwing of silk became established as a domestic industry at Coventry, Leicester, Derby, Macclesfield and, by the end of the eighteenth century, was spreading beyond Manchester.

Several hand-driven and pedal machines were used in the throwing of silk and preparing it for the loom; they were housed in the homes or workshops of the throwsters. Sometimes the merchants who supplied the raw silk also provided the machines and in these circumstances it was found more convenient to have special premises called 'throwing houses'. Here the throwsters worked under supervision and were paid by the piece, that is, for the amount of work done. In a throwing-house the employer could keep an eye on the silk, a valuable material which was liable to disappear if the workers were not honest.

Throwing-houses were quite small places, sometimes an old barn or cowhouse, but they were a step towards the factory or mill or engineering shop, buildings where work-people are paid wages to 'mind' machines. The next step was the introduction of power to work the machines. For many centuries men had used water as a source of power. Streams turned wheels which were geared to two large flat stones; as the wheel turned the stones rotated; corn was trickled between them and was ground to flour. The flour-mill was a familiar sight in most villages. A few other ways of using water-power had also been contrived, for example, the fulling-mill; water-power was used in several of the processes in preparing metals but, until the eighteenth century, its use was very restricted.

In 1718, a machine for throwing silk driven by water-power was introduced into England by John Lombe of Derby. Lombe had stolen the idea from Italy. He had worked there on similar machines, pretending to be an apprentice, but his real purpose was to learn how the machines were constructed. He brought drawings back to England, built a factory on an island in the Derwent near Derby and installed throwing-machines, using the river for power. It was said that he employed 200 workers. There is a tradition that Lombe was followed to Derby by an Italian who stabbed him to death in revenge for his theft of the invention. His brother carried on the business of the throwing-mill.

In time throwing-mills run by water-power were erected in other towns. Charles Rowe built one in Macclesfield and the town became famous for the manufacture of silk. Throwing silk by machinery stimulated the weaving side of the industry by providing cheaper and more plentiful supplies of thread. It proved to be so efficient and labour-saving that many men tried their hand at inventing a similar machine to spin wool and cotton but this was not accomplished successfully until fifty years after the opening of the mill at Derby.

Meanwhile changes were taking place in the production of woollen and cotton goods similar to those which led to the establishment of throwing-houses for silk. Increasingly the tools and hand-driven machines were provided by an employer who assembled them in factories where workers could be organized and supervised. In pot- and glass-making and in many other industries the domestic system altered until the domestic worker was dependent on a merchant for his raw material and for the sale of his goods and sometimes for the machines on which he worked. Only one further example will be given— the manufacture of iron and steel and the products made from these metals. This has been chosen because there was great variation in the development of the different branches of the industry.

Some processes of metal manufacture did not lend themselves to domestic production so, as far as is known, iron and steel-making has for many hundreds of years been organized as it is today in workshops where iron-workers work for wages paid by an employer. The scale of operations has increased enormously, the methods of iron-making have been altered and greatly improved but there has been no change in the structure of the industry.

On the other hand, the making of iron commodities, nails, kettles, pans, fire-irons and so on was, in the eighteenth century, an excellent example of the domestic system and also of the changes that prepared the way for the industrial revolution. Moreover, one branch of iron-fashioning, the making of horseshoes, has remained to this day what it always must have been, a customer–producer relationship. Horseshoes cannot be bought in shops in sizes as shoes for humans are bought; they are made in the forge and fashioned to the horse's hoof by a smith. The customer, not of course the horse but the horse's owner, pays the smith and there the transaction ends. The producer of the horseshoe is in direct contact with the man who buys it. Systems of production seldom cease entirely. Vestiges of older ways linger.

In early times iron was smelted by the use of charcoal which needs, for its preparation, great quantities of wood. For this reason, although ironstone was to be found in many counties of England, the first furnaces were placed where wood was available, in or near forests such as the Sussex Weald and the Forest of Dean or on the outskirts of the Lake District. The casting of iron into moulds was generally done by men employed by ironmasters but there were exceptions. Isaac Wilkinson, the founder of a great family of ironmasters, started in a small way by carrying molten iron in ladles from a blast furnace across the road to his foundry where, by casting, he made it into pots, pans and kettles. These he sold to the owners of the blast furnace. This was at Backbarrow near Morecambe Bay and can almost be described as a domestic industry.

Nevertheless, it is in the manufacture of iron into small articles such as nails, tools, chains and the metal furnishings of harness, bits, bridles and spurs that the true domestic industry can be seen. Bars of iron were supplied by the ironmaster and were worked in forges which were either part of the smith's home or built in his yard. Many of these small iron workshops can still be seen in the iron-fields of England, Worcester, Sheffield and in south Derbyshire, for example. Men and women worked together, stripped to the waist in the heat of the forge. In chain-making, as the chain lengthened it was coiled round the body and the coil thickened as link was added to link. It was a thirsty job and gallons of ale were consumed in the course of a day. The finished goods were sold either to a merchant who took them to market or to the provider of the iron who sold them wholesale.

As the timber in the forests was exhausted, the iron industry became more and more scattered and, by the eighteenth century, could be found far from the iron-fields. In search of woodland, the industry migrated to North Wales, Cheshire, North Lancashire and Scotland, wherever, indeed, wood was still to be found. The shortage of timber hampered the iron industry as early as the sixteenth century; by the eighteenth, the shortage was acute and the very existence of the industry was threatened. Yet the demand for iron was increasing rapidly, not only for the traditional uses but also for guns and cannons which were being increasingly used in war.

Beneath the bridge at the loch end of the Pass of Branden in Argyll, the river runs over masses of slag, the reject of eighteenth-century furnaces put into blast with the timber from the now almost tree-less Ben Cruachan. Here, too, are the ruined smelting-houses and the remains of the ironworkers' cottages. The ironstone was brought by sea and loch from Cumberland. The smelted iron bars either made the same journey in reverse or were carried by pack ponies over the hilly rough roads to the towns of Scotland and England. Such long and difficult hauls were troublesome and expensive. It became essential, if the iron industry were to survive, to find an alternative to charcoal for smelting.

Coal, though suitable for forging, cannot be used

2 Hand-loom silk weavers in a weaving garret (see p. 15)

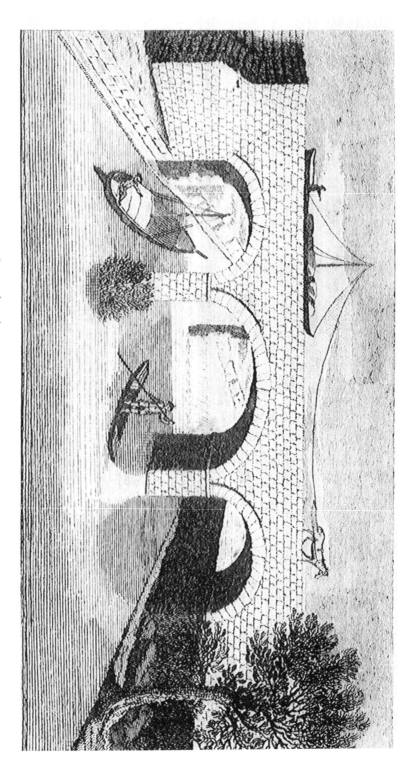

3. *Bridgewater canal aqueduct (see p. 44)*

in its raw state for smelting. After many trials and failures it was found that coke, which is made from coal, was an excellent alternative for this purpose. Abraham Darby, an ironmaster in Coalbrookdale, Shropshire, was the first successfully to smelt iron with coke. The story goes that, after many disappointments, he watched the furnace for six days and six nights in sleepless vigilance. Then, seeing the metal from the coke-fired ore flow free and pure, he was carried away exhausted and unconscious. This story and others concerning Abraham's discoveries and improvements were told by his wife and daughter; the thrill and excitement come to us through the years between. Mrs. Darby wrote, 'Had not these discoveries been made the iron trade of our own produce would have dwindled, for woods for charcoal became very scarce and landed gentlemen rose the prices of wood exceeding high. Indeed it would not have been to be got.'

Coke smelting was one of the most important steps towards making the industrial revolution possible. The earlier power-driven machines were made of wood, sometimes reinforced by iron at the points of greatest strain. As iron cheapened and became more plentiful it was used to make the entire machine, other inventions and improvements were made on the eve of the industrial revolution towards toughening iron and making it into steel. In many of these processes water-power took the place of human muscle. The great hammers which beat the iron were driven by water-power and so also were the bellows which blew the furnace and the shears which cut the iron into sheets.

So, by the middle of the eighteenth century, there had been many changes in the way goods were made and already there were signs that the use of more complicated machines and the use of power were altering the structure of industry. The new methods could not be economically adopted by the average domestic worker. They needed large capital outlay and teams of work-people working under supervision for regular hours. Why is this so important that, when it became the general rule, it is called a revolution?

The way in which people earn their living and the relationships between the people engaged—owner, worker, organizer, buyer, seller and so on, have a far-reaching influence on society. The domestic system of manufacture changed the nature of much of the countryside, altering the purely rural village, concerned only with agriculture, into a farming-industrial unit. It created industrial hamlets where before had been moorland or rough pasture. It changed the balance of population, filling up areas which had previously been all but empty. It enlarged places like Manchester, Birmingham and Leeds from small market towns to large bustling centres of trade and industry. Domestic industries set hundreds of thousands of pack-horses on the trot along ancient tracks which deepened into troughs with the impact. New ports, such as Liverpool, were created from marshes to bring in raw material and send out finished goods. In old ports, London, Bristol, Newcastle, Portsmouth, new docks were built to cope with the increased volume of trade.

The industrial revolution was to have even more far-reaching effects on society than the domestic system. It has produced many of the differences between the present time and the eighteenth century. In order to appreciate these differences, it is necessary to look a little more closely at life in the earlier period. Many of the industrial workers of the eighteenth century had small holdings of land. They kept a cow or two, a horse and a pig. They grew a little corn, rye or oats which was ground into flour at the local mill. They brewed their own ale and baked bread or made oatcakes. This made for independence and versatility. In the Heywood home at Little Lever, when weaving ran short there was the farm to be tended or work to be done in the carpenter's shop.

Freedom and independence from the age-long deference to landlord or squire, who dominated the rural village, made for independence in habit and thought. For example, the tenants and agricultural labourers in a rural village were expected to attend the Church of England for the parson was often related to the squire. It is noticeable that Nonconformist chapels and Quaker Meeting Houses flourished most in areas where domestic industries were practised. During the industrial revolution, it was this

25

spirit of independence that made it difficult to adjust to the new discipline of regular hours, confinement in a factory and dependence on an employer for work. The domestic industry workers were not accustomed to fitting their work into a set pattern. They would, if they felt so inclined, work long into the night, taking the next day off for other jobs or for a spree.

It would be a mistake to look at the domestic system through rose-coloured glasses, though many people have idealized it and, during the early industrial revolution, the period was remembered with longing. Nevertheless, there were serious drawbacks. The amount of goods that could be produced by hand was very small and this meant that the standard of living for the mass of the population was low in comparison with our own. Dresses and underwear, stockings, suits and boots had to last for many years and they were patched and darned as they wore thin. A 'best' gown would be expected to last a lifetime. It was handed down from mother to daughter and only worn on special occasions. Household goods were expensive and, rather than replace them, they would be repaired. Pokers were taken to the blacksmith to be retipped, shovels had their edges renewed and tinkers travelled about the country filling the holes in pots and pans.

Houses were simply furnished. It was recorded as a mark of high prosperity that weavers had a chest of drawers and a grandfather clock in the house-place (living-room-kitchen), a tea service of china instead of the older wooden plates and horn beakers and flagged floors instead of beaten earth. Floors were sanded for cleanliness and warmth and there would be a home-made rag rug in front of the fire. Many thousands of domestic workers had no more comfort than this and many thousands had less. The fact that industry was carried on in the home entailed a certain amount of dirt and disorder, more or less according to the type of work done. The iron-worker's home must have been impossible to keep clean, the textile worker's less so, though the fluff from wool, silk or cotton would be pervasive.

One of the greatest difficulties that hampered and restricted the domestic industries was the problem of transport. Few new roads had been made in England since the Romans were here many hundreds of years ago. Many Roman roads were still in use, for example, the great north road to Scotland and the road from London to Chester. Little had been done for their repair and they were badly battered by the wear of the centuries. Such new roads as there were in the eighteenth century had not been specially constructed, they were ancient tracks which had been widened and the surface hardened by the padding of countless horses' hoofs or the feet of men.

Along these roads bolts of cloth, metal-ware, pots and coal had to be gathered from the widespread hamlets and taken to the towns. If the goods were for export to Europe or England's new colonies, they must make a further journey to the seaports. Transport was mainly by pack-horse but great lumbering wagons came increasingly into use. Their heavy wheels ground into the surface of the roads and made deep ruts which widened into holes big enough to bring traffic to a standstill in wet weather. Records of the eighteenth century resound with the cries of distress from travellers complaining of the condition of the roads.

Some attempt was made at improving them by creating turnpike trusts. Stretches of road were taken over by groups of individuals who found the money for improvement by surfacing and straightening. In return, a charge was made for the use of the road, so much for a horse and rider, so much for a wagon or coach, so much for cattle and sheep, in sums ranging from 1d. to 2s. Toll-houses, where the charge was collected are still to be seen on many British roads. There are several on A.5, London to Holyhead. They are generally many sided so that the toll-keeper could look in all directions and be in readiness to open the toll bar to travellers without delay. Mr. Pickwick's man-servant, Sam Weller, in *Pickwick Papers* said that toll-keepers were a melancholy and dismal lot, bored doubtless by the monotony of the job.

The England of the eighteenth century contained, of course, many people who were not concerned directly in the domestic industries and who were little affected by them except that more goods were available for them to buy. The population in 1750 was estimated as being round about six million persons (there are no precise population figures for any time before 1801, when the first census was taken). Our present population (1966) is nearly fifty millions, over eight times as many.

At the top of the social scale there was a small group of wealthy landowners, perhaps about a couple of thousand families. At the lower end of the scale there were about a million families where the bread-winner was either an agricultural labourer or in a poorly paid job, such as attending to the many horses, peddling smallware, domestic service or rough cleaning. The people in this class were barely able to keep themselves and their families. They could not save. When out of work, ill or old they quickly became destitute. Most of them, at some time or another, 'came on the parish', that is, received public relief.

In between the rich and the poor were the farmers and smallholders, professional men, such as doctors, clergymen and lawyers and also the merchants, craftsmen and the workers in the domestic industries. Of all these farmers who farmed their own land were by far the largest group. Because many farmers also engaged in industry, it is difficult to disentangle the two groups. At a guess which will not be too far out, over one-third of the population depended in some degree on agriculture for all or part of their living. Two-thirds lived in the country.

In the half-century before the industrial revolution the yield from the land had been increasing. New methods of cultivation such as sowing seeds in drills instead of broadcast, avoided waste and made weeding easier. A new field crop, the turnip, was introduced which fed cattle in winter and so enabled the whole herd to be kept alive instead of, as formerly, only a small proportion. This was a most important innovation; it was mainly the work of Charles Townshend, 'Turnip Townshend' as he was nicknamed. Before the inclusion of turnips in a rotation, one-third of the land had been left fallow to 'rest' after two successive corn crops. This was no longer necessary for turnips restored the land and also checked weeds by smothering them with a dense growth of leaves. The cultivation of turnips, therefore, increased the number of cattle and increased the crop-yield from the land.

During the eighteenth century some of the profits and rents from agricultural land were invested in trade and industry and, conversely, some of the profits of trade were used to improve the land. One result of this fruitful inter-relation was the building of the 'stately homes', many of which are now open to the public. It is usual to find, in the history of the families who built them, some increase in income from investment in, say, shipping which carried metal or textiles to the West Indies and brought back sugar or rum. Many landed estates contained coal or iron mines which the landowners leased and from which they obtained royalties—payments per ton on the metal raised. Many landowners, perhaps the majority, increased their estates by the enclosure of common land.

Over much of England, land had been cultivated for hundreds of years in large open fields in which the villagers had a varying number of intermingling strips. Surrounding the village were stretches of pasture and rough grazing for cattle where villagers and landlord had rights of use in common with each other. There was also an area of 'waste', land not always distinguishable from pasture but generally rougher and having trees, bushes or peat upon it. Waste provided fuel, wild fruits and a run for pigs, cattle and horses. Rights on the waste were less defined than rights in the common fields and pasture. This is an England that is gone except at Laxton, Nottinghamshire, where an example is preserved under the National Trust.

It was found that the open field and common system of agricultural organization did not fit in with the new agricultural methods and that improvements were difficult to apply, since all had to agree before they could even be tried. So, in thousands of parishes the open field system was abandoned and the present landscape of farm-houses surrounded by fields enclosed by hedges or walls began to take shape. In all about fourteen million acres were enclosed. The process began before the period of the industrial revolution and continued through it and the two were closely inter-connected. Many countrymen and women left the land after the enclosures and went to work in the new industrial districts. The new methods of farming provided food for the increased population. The increase in population was possible because of the increased amount of food grown by the new methods. The industrial revolution provided more people with money to buy food. Agricultural and industrial change were dependent on one another.

3

A New Method of Transport

DURING the period of the industrial revolution the population of Britain not only increased but also became differently distributed. Previously, London and the rich agricultural counties of the south and east had the greatest number of people to the square mile. In the eighteenth century more and more people moved to the new industrial districts—the iron-fields of the midlands and Yorkshire, the textile districts of the West Riding and south-east Lancashire. Further changes took place within these areas as the industrial revolution developed. Then, as now, people sought work where it was to be found.

An example of this is the village of Rainow, on one of the hills which separate Cheshire from Derbyshire. In the eighteenth century the villagers spun and wove silk and cotton in their homes and grazed sheep and cattle on Rainow Knoll, a rounded hill near by. Rainow Knoll was enclosed; factories using water-power were built along the stream in the valley below the village. For a while the villagers worked in the factories and climbed back to their homes when the day's work was over. Then, when steam took the place of water for driving the machines, factories were built in towns near or on the coal-fields. The census of 1831 records a decrease in population at Rainow and offers as an explanation in a marginal note that many of the inhabitants had left Rainow to seek work in the cotton-manufacturing towns such as Stockport or Manchester. Both these towns had coal-mines near their boundaries.

In earlier times coal was gathered from the surface or hewn out of the seams where they outcropped. Coal is bulky and heavy to transport, the cheapest and easiest way of moving it was by water carriage. At Newcastle-on-Tyne the coal seams came to the surface on the sea-shore and, therefore, Newcastle had the advantage of easily mined coal and easy transport. Coal was sent to London by sea during the Middle Ages; to distinguish it from charcoal, it was called 'sea coal'. The old saying, 'It is no use sending coals to Newcastle' reflects the abundance of coal sent from that town.

Gradually, coal-mining spread to other districts where coal outcropped or could be got from shallow pits or by making tunnels into a hillside. Mining villages grew round the coal pits. Because of the difficulty of transport most of the early coal-fields were developed only when they were near the sea or a navigable river, though many small inland mines supplied a local demand. Coal was not yet in general use for house-warming or cooking; wood or charcoal was preferred as being cleaner but, from the sixteenth century onward, coal was in increasing demand for brewing ale, boiling soap, making salt, dyeing cloth and in forging. The remains of small inland mines opened to supply a local industry are to be found in the most unlikely places—the hills or Shropshire, the Pennines and Wales—pits and tunnels, long since abandoned, the ruined huts of the miners covered with the growth of centuries.

In coal-mining changes of location followed increasing skill in mining the deeper beds of coal. As the seams near the surface became exhausted it was necessary to mine deeper or find new coal-fields. Both these measures were adopted. By the end of the sixteenth century mines were already two hundred feet deep and many new mines were opened. They were worked by gangs of men who, together, leased the mine from the landholder. The coal was brought to the surface in baskets up a series of ladders and the problems of draining and boring had created a new type of specialist—the mining bailiff, a forerunner of the mining engineer.

The owner of a new mine near a navigable river was fortunate. Anne Newdigate's husband had mines in Warwickshire, through which the River Avon runs. Her cousin, who wrote to her from London in 1603, urged her to come to town to see the Coronation of James I. 'London streets shall be handed with cloth of gold when the king cometh. . . . Either come up now and see all this bravery or close your eyes

35

while you live and let Jack's colepits pay for all.'
Anne did not go; she would not leave her children.
She did, however, have many fine gowns and jewels
from the profits of her husband's 'colepits'.

By the eighteenth century the development of the
coal industry was seriously hampered by the cost
and difficulty of transport. The altered pattern of
population and the siting of industries in regions previously mainly agricultural took place within a
framework of road and river transport which had
been intended to meet very different circumstances.
Strenuous efforts were made to improve the rivers by
deepening and straightening and by providing tow-
paths and locks. The navigable length of most of the
rivers of England was increased considerably. The
turnpike-road system was extended and many ways
were tried to improve the surface so that it could
take heavy traffic without disintegrating. None of
these efforts was adequate to meet the need.

The rivers in the new industrial districts were short
and shallow. Even when improved there was often a
long road-haul for goods produced inland. No surface was as yet devised which could withstand the
pounding of wagon wheels and, moreover, road
carriage was expensive. An eight-horse wagon carried
only about a ton of goods between twenty and thirty
miles a day and required a man and a boy to drive it.
A new means of transport was urgently needed.

Canals, which could provide a man-made system
of water carriage were the eighteenth-century solu-

tion to the problem. The experience which had been gained in improving rivers provided a starting point, for many short lengths of artificial river beds or 'cuts' had been built to straighten bends. Many rivers were almost 'canalized' but, there was one important difference: a river provides its own head of water; a canal gets its water from reservoirs by 'feeders', small canals.

The first canals were built to carry coal. 'A canal must have coal at the heels of it', said the Duke of Bridgewater, who built the first canal and many others. It is true that no other commodity was so profitable to the canal owners but the new waterways were so cheap and convenient that a mounting volume of goods was carried along them. Many people used them as an alternative to horseback or coach-riding for there was no horse to be stabled at the end of the journey—'no parking problem', as we should say and it was cheaper than the coach. During the industrial revolution whole families with their household goods and furniture travelled by canal from the rural villages of the south in search of work in the mills and factories of the north of England.

Francis Egerton, Duke of Bridgewater, the 'Founder of inland navigation' had an unusual and surprising life. He was the only survivor in a family of more than a dozen children and he was so sickly that he was not expected to live. It was not thought worth while to educate him and he was left to the care of servants and stable-lads. His mother took a dislike to him. When he was 12 years old, his father and all his brothers having died, he became the heir to large estates in several parts of England. It was necessary to 'groom' him for the dukedom. He was almost illiterate and, as might be expected, uncouth and awkward from neglect. It was even thought that he was mentally deficient.

He was sent to Eton where he was birched, bullied and very unhappy. At 18 years of age he was provided with a private tutor and sent to travel on the continent of Europe. His tutor seems to have understood and sympathized with him and the sunny climate of Italy cleared up his lung trouble and strengthened his constitution. At 21 years of age he succeeded to the title and estates. He was now tall, well-made, in reasonable health and with a fair amount of education. But he never recovered from his neglected childhood, being shy and inelegant in company and, perhaps because he felt himself to be at a disadvantage, given to bouts of drinking.

For a while he lived the life of a man-about-town. He gambled, kept race-horses and made the acquaintance of fashionable London. He became engaged to marry a beautiful and lively girl who did not love him but who was prepared to marry him for his money and position. This engagement was soon broken and the Duke, to escape the gossip and condolences of his circle of acquaintances, retreated to his Lancashire estate at Worsley, about six miles north-west of Manchester. Here there was an Elizabethan mansion, some farm-land and a coal-mine.

Coal from the mine was taken to Manchester in panniers slung from the backs of pack-horses. The cost of getting it there was twice as much as the cost of getting it out of the mine. The Duke became interested and then immersed in the problem of providing water-carriage to cut the cost and also to allow of greater quantities being moved in one load. At first he thought of using a small stream, the Worsley Brook, but the head of water was too small. His later decision to build a canal was the commencement of his life's work as a canal builder. It is not too much to say that it was a revolutionary decision, for canals changed the face of England and had far-reaching consequences for industrial and social life.

Two other men were concerned in this great undertaking—John Gilbert and James Brindley. John Gilbert was the Duke's estate agent. He had been trained as an engineer under Matthew Boulton who, together with James Watt, launched the steam engine. John Gilbert was largely responsible for the accounting side of the business. He bought the materials needed for building the canals and paid the workers. James Brindley was a farm-labourer's son who had left home rather than work on the land. He had a taste and talent for machinery and he persuaded a millwright, Abraham Bennett, to allow him to 'make himself useful about the workshop' in return for food and lodgings. Young Brindley made himself so useful that his master apprenticed him to the trade without the usual premium, at that time a great benefit to a

D

penniless youngster. Bennett occasionally 'went on a spree' for two or three days' hard drinking and in his absence Bridley would take charge of the work in hand. Brindley became known as a skilful and reliable craftsman. He showed great originality in dealing with the problem of water in mines on hillsides by draining the water by means of ditches cut to an opening below the coal seams. He could hardly read or write; his notebooks contain ill-spelt words written in a scrawl, the sentences incomplete and ungrammatical; for example, 'To masurin Duks pools atin and drink 6d.'

Under the Duke, Brindley supervised the day-to-day building of the canals, organizing the workmen and dealing with practical problems as they arose for though 'clever with his hands', he had little theoretical knowledge. When faced with a difficulty which he could not immediately solve, he retired to bed with a jug of water and a loaf of bread and stayed there until he found the solution 'in his head'. He is credited with the introduction of 'puddling' to make the bed of the canal watertight. Puddling was done by pounding clay as a lining for the cut; the workmen used their feet to do this.

These three men, the Duke, shy and awkward but wealthy and imaginative, John Gilbert, a steady and competent manager and a good man of business, James Brindley, rough, unlettered but with a practical talent almost amounting to genius, made an excellent team. They agreed well and their abilities supplemented each other. Gilbert and Brindley had rooms in the Hall at Worsley and often, in the press of work, they would share a simple meal with the Duke. A nice distinction of degree was observed. The Duke was 'Your Grace'; John Gilbert was 'Mr. Gilbert'; Brindley was simply 'James'.

Gilbert was particular about his clothes and always managed to look spruce. Brindley clung to an old, long, grey coat and a battered hat and could not be persuaded to discard them. He rode an old nag to which he was much attached and would not change her even when her speed had long gone. He lived very simply and saved most of his wages which accumulated in a leather bag. As the canal schemes grew larger and needed more capital, the Duke was often short of ready money to pay the workmen's wages. Brindley would then produce his bag and lend the Duke a hundred pounds or so.

The Duke's part in the enterprise was to find the money, ensure the passing of the Parliamentary Bills necessary to the building of the canals and to negotiate with the owners of the land through which the canals passed. As head of the undertaking, he made the final decisions. He was particularly good in keeping workmen and staff in good heart and temper. He could infect them with his own enthusiasm. This was very necessary with the workmen who were faced, on a project new and strange, with hard, dirty and unaccustomed work. Labourers on the Worsley estate supplemented by other local men dug the first canal but, as the Duke's canals spread over England, a specialized force was recruited, many of them Irish immigrants. They were called 'navvies' because they built 'navigations', an alternative term for canals or waterways.

The Duke, when making an inspection of the work in progress would drop into familiar conversation with the navvies and they would reply in like manner. On one occasion he was congratulating a father on a brood of fine children and the birth of another. The Duke, who never married, wished that he, too, had a family. '*I wish*', said the workman, 'that you had half of my children and I had half of your money.' The Duke roared with laughter and left the man a coin to 'wet the baby's head'. The Duke would order beer for men on unusually hard or difficult stretches of the cuts and he would reward good and sustained effort with extra pay. When a section of the work was completed he would order a supper of beef, pudding and beer to be served to the men and, when a canal was completed a more lavish spread was provided with toasts, singing and dancing. He was, it seems, happier in such simple company than in the drawing-rooms of London.

The Bridgewater Canal was commenced in 1759, when the Duke was 23, Gilbert 35 and Brindley 43 years of age. These three men, so different in age, background and temperament, worked together for thirteen years. Together they built over 365 miles of canals including the Bridgewater, the Trent and

Mersey and its extension, and the Grand Trunk. Brindley, who was the oldest and who bore the brunt of the fieldwork, died as the result of a heavy cold aggravated by years of overwork at the age of 56. After his death the Duke went on building canals for a few years but the French wars in the last decade of the eighteenth century and the death of Gilbert, in 1795, put an end to new projects. The Duke lived to be 67; he died in 1803.

Although there was great difficulty in raising money for his schemes, the early canals were a financial success and the Duke made a fortune. He spent some of it in making a collection of pictures and porcelain. He became a patron of artists, in particular the young Turner, whose pictures he bought before they became fashionable and while Turner was struggling for public recognition. The Duke built a new hall at Worsley and, when England was at war with France, he subscribed £100,000 to the public funds, a sum equal to about one million today. Thus the neglected and disregarded child became famous and respected and had the good fortune to find work of importance to which he was well suited and which kept him busy and happy for forty years.

The Bridgewater Canal fired public imagination not only because it was the first to be built but also because of certain ingenious features in its construction. In order to reach Manchester from Worsley it was necessary to cross the River Irwell. High embankments were built across the valley and the canal was carried on an aqueduct over the river. This was considered a marvel and was internationally famous. People came to see it from the continent of Europe. Pictures drawn at the time show parties of fashionably dressed ladies and gentlemen standing astonished at the sight of sailing-boats on the canal floating high above ships on the river. It was said that ladies fainted at the spectacle and that gentlemen bled from the nose. House parties of 'gentry' from neighbouring halls came to see the aqueduct and took a trip on the canal. Lord Stamford of Dunham Massey brought one such party. They were entertained by the Duke and a 'cold Collation' was provided on board. Large numbers of people in humbler circumstances lined the banks watching the boats. As with time the raw banks greened over, the tow-paths became a favourite promenade.

The canal, however, was not built to provide a spectacle; its function was to carry the Duke's coal. Once on the canal, transit was easy. Hauling coal from the coal-face to the surface was tedious and slow for it had to be done along narrow, low passages which were running with water. Water-logged mines were a serious problem at this period. A solution was found that solved the two problems of transit and drainage. A subterranean canal was driven through the Worsley mine, with branches, thirty miles in all. The coal was loaded into barges at the coal-face from raised platforms and was then pushed to the mine opening by poles. Here, the barges

44

entered the canal without the necessity of unloading and reloading. The contrivance for hoisting coal from the different mine levels was very ingenious. The all too abundant water in the mine was used as a counter-weight to carry an endless chain of buckets to the required height. The coal went up as the water came down. Water from the mines also fed the canal though, as there was not always a sufficiency, a reservoir was provided, using the Worsley Brook. These various devices were another source of interest to visitors who, having sailed along the aqueduct, took an underground trip into the mine.

The canal, which was called the Bridgewater navigation, was opened in 1761 and was subsequently extended to Runcorn where it entered the Mersey by a series of locks. This extension passed through several towns whose commercial centre was Manchester. A passenger service was offered. The following is an extract from a handbill issued at the time:

Daily service from Altrincham to Manchester.
Fast Flyboats leave Altrincham Wharf daily at 7.0 a.m.
Elegant breakfasts served on board.
Return 6.0. p.m. from Gaythorn Lock.

This service was continued until 1850 when it ceased owing to the competition of the newly established railways.

The success of the Bridgewater was immediate for the cost of carriage on the canal was half that of the road. The price of coal in Manchester was reduced from 1s. to 4d. a cwt. Moreover, large quantities of goods could be carried in one load over districts hitherto only served by pack-horses. The Duke's enterprise had opened possibilities of cheap, easy water-transport to inland industrial areas remote from navigable rivers. A canal was of particular advantage to industries requiring coal or producing bulky products.

The pottery industry of Staffordshire was in just such a situation. Large quantities of coal were used to bake the clay; pots are bulky and fragile so there were considerable breakage losses when jogged over the rough roads of the time. A few years before the Duke built the Bridgewater, a new kind of clay had been introduced into the making of ceramics. This clay was only to be found in Cornwall, 200 miles from Staffordshire.

For centuries earthenware had been made in the district round Stoke-on-Trent, using the local clay. For this reason the area is called 'The Potteries'. Josiah Wedgwood, born in 1730, was one of a family of potters who had been making earthenware for several generations. Josiah worked as a youth at the potter's wheel in his father's workshop. He had an inventive turn of mind and made several experimental mixtures, trying to improve and refine the clay. When he was 21 years old he and his cousin Thomas opened a small pot-works near Stoke and here he succeeded in producing a finer type of earthenware and designed a variety of models for the workmen to copy and bake.

46

Porcelain or China, so called because it was first made in that country, lends itself to more delicate and intricate decoration than the coarser earthenware. Josiah Wedgwood went to Italy where he saw and greatly admired the beautiful and elegantly decorated vases and urns which remained from the ancient civilizations of the Etruscan, Greek and Roman people. He brought back sketches and specimens and used them to produce a new and superior style of ceramics which became very fashionable. Still seeking to improve the clay mixture, he transported the fine white clay which had recently been discovered in Cornwall but this meant a long and expensive road haul across Cheshire as well as transport by sea from Cornwall to Liverpool.

Josiah Wedgwood and the Duke of Bridgewater were acquainted. Wedgwood had followed the progress of the Duke's canal with interest and was present at its opening and shortly afterwards, on Wedgwood's instigation, the Trent and Mersey Canal was planned and building commenced. The Trent and Mersey connected the two rivers by a waterway across Cheshire into Staffordshire. It was built by the Duke and financed partly by him and partly by Wedgwood. Wedgwood established an entirely new pottery on the banks of the canal and built a house for himself and cottages for his workpeople. This new settlement was called Etruria, because it was from the Etruscan people of ancient times that he had received inspiration for his designs. Clay

47

and coal could now be brought along the canal and delivered to the work's quay, a great saving of time, labour and money. Wedgwood used the clay from Cornwall to make the china or porcelain for which he became famous. 'Wedgwood' became a household word. He was appointed potter to the Queen in 1762.

Other canals followed until most of England and some parts of Scotland and Wales were within easy reach of a network of inland waterways. The main rivers were connected. Indeed, canal-building became a mania and many canals were built which were a financial failure owing to insufficient carriage of heavy goods. Although the first canal was acclaimed, later canals roused strong opposition for those who had invested money in improving the rivers feared the competition of the canals and those employed on road and river transport saw a menace to their livelihood. Landowners resisted the passage of the canals through their land, objecting to the disturbance of rural life occasioned by the presence of 'drunken and dissolute bargees', who, it was said, would commit all sorts of crimes and be off down the canal before they could be caught. Later promoters of canals met opposition from the Duke, who fought hard and often successfully to prevent waterways being created which would compete with his own. The Duke's power was feared. It was said, 'A monopoly in the hand of a peer would be such a monster as I hope this land of liberty will never suffer to live.'

After the Duke of Bridgewater the most famous

canal builder was Thomas Telford. He was the son of a shepherd and worked as a mason in Dumfries-shire, his birthplace. As a youth he wrote poetry, some of which was published and praised. He worked at his trade in Edinburgh and, in 1782, when he was 25 years of age, he went to London. He did some work for various local authorities and became known as a competent engineer and surveyor. He built many canals of which the most remarkable is the Ellesmere and its extension to Llangollen. This canal is carried high above the Ceiriog valley at Chirk on an aqueduct of great beauty and dignity. One of his greatest engineering feats was the construction of the Caledonian Canal which, using the series of lochs that almost cut across Scotland, made them into a continuous waterway.

Telford also built or reconstructed many thousands of miles of road, devising a firm type of foundation and a method of draining that increased their durability. He also built bridges and a church at Bridgnorth, one of the few churches of the period. This church, like all of Telford's work, has the austere shapeliness of good engineering. The poetic sensibility of his youth and his taste for literature were transmuted into a calm beauty peculiar to his creations. This characteristic is particularly seen in the suspension bridge over the Menai Strait, connecting Anglesey with the mainland of Wales. One of his latest works was the Macclesfield canal which, in miniature, shows Telford's skill in dealing with unusual problems. One of the bridges is built on the skew to avoid creating an awkward bend on the road above. The stones of the bridge are placed with consummate artifice.

In all, 3,000 miles of canal were built. The gradient of the land was a major factor in influencing the route. Locks, which are enclosures with gates at either end, are the device used to lower and lift boats as they pass from level to level. They are time-wasting and sometimes it was thought better to avoid making them by carrying the canal along a detour. The early canal builders, especially Brindley, were not expert at lock construction and did not like making them. 'Water is a giant,' he said, 'but the giant must be laid flat on his back.' A tunnel through a hill was an alternative to locks. Along these tunnels the canal-men or bargees lay on their backs on the boat and, with their feet on the roof of the tunnel, 'walked' along, taking the barge with them. This was called 'legging the boat' and, through long tunnels, the wives and older children of the bargees helped the men. One such tunnel at Harecastle in Staffordshire, was a mile and a half long. Progress was at the rate of one mile an hour. The tow-horses were walked round the hill and rejoined the barge at the other end of the tunnel.

On the canal which went from Lancashire to Yorkshire, locks and a tunnel were both used to get through the Pennines. A series of locks like a flight of stairs carries the boats part way up the hill; the next stage is a tunnel through the hill and a second flight of locks on the other side completes the journey. This tunnel is 3 miles 130 yards long. Many hours and a great deal of effort were expended even if the way were clear; if there were a queue of barges, a day would be wasted in waiting.

Locks, tunnels and the plodding pace of the barge-horse made canal transport slow. In the early years of the nineteenth century small steam engines were tried to increase speed. Unfortunately, they were not successful, for the canal banks were not designed to stand the strong wash of water produced by the transit of fast boats. The banks leaked or broke away and had constantly to be repaired. In winter the waterway was liable to freeze and barges would be held up, waiting for a thaw. Canals were built in differing widths so that the larger boats could not enter the smaller canals. Goods had to be un-loaded and transferred. Nevertheless, in spite of these and other difficulties, for heavy cargoes canals were an immense improvement on the roads of the period.

As the industrial revolution 'got into its stride' they became less and less adequate to carry the growing volume of goods. A better method of transport was urgently needed. This need was met by the steam locomotive and the railway. Rail or 'tramway' tracks as they were called had been in use for some time. Horse-drawn wagons carried coal along them from the coal-face; they were used for the transit of goods from one place to another in ironworks; several miles of tramway had been laid to bring limestone from Derbyshire to the Peak Forest Canal. The Duke of Bridgewater regarded tramways as a menace to his navigations. With unusual foresight, he could see their advantage over waterways if the steam engine could be adapted for locomotion. Towards the end of his life the Duke said, 'Canals will last my lifetime but what I fear is those damned tramways.'

When the canal system was established, the people who worked the boats became a separate and distinct community—a race apart. They have been called 'water-gypsies' because they were constantly on the move and because their means of transport were also their homes. They were a rough and tough people, rather looked down on as being ignorant and un-trustworthy. Because they had no settled home it was not possible for their children to go to school so that, as a class, they were even more unlettered than other workers in eighteenth-century England.

Usually, a family worked two barges, 'a pair of boats', each boat loaded with about forty tons. There was a tiny cabin on each boat, 10 ft. by 7 ft. with so little head-room that it was not possible to stand upright and even sitting had to be done with care lest the head bumped against the ceiling. In one cabin the cooking was done and here husband, wife and small children slept. The older children slept in the cabin on the after-boat. Most of the time the family would be on deck or walking along the tow-path but in bad weather or sickness the only shelter was the squalid cabin. Thousands of babies were born in such cramped quarters.

Bargee families were accused of many crimes, probably often through prejudice, but drunkenness, thieving and dirtiness seem to have been fairly common. It was difficult to be fastidious in such conditions; cold and exposure would lead to hard drinking; clothes drying on a hedge, eggs and hens from secluded hen-runs and similar unguarded property could easily be picked up and carried down canal before the owners were aware of their loss. More serious charges were made of loss by pilfering of the goods carried.

Within themselves, the bargees were a close-knit and loyal fraternity. They stood by each other, helped each other and knew each other well if working the same routes, and by repute from over a wide area. Ale houses specially catering for the canal folk were to be found at intervals near or along the waterways. They were often called 'The Navigation' or 'The Navigators' Rest' or the 'Barge Pole'. Some of these inns were opened to serve the navvies who built the canal and remained to serve the watermen. Here, warmth, a rough meal, drink, shelter, and convivial company whiled away the time waiting turn for the lock or between unloading and reloading. The inn was a clearing-house for information about conditions on the canals and gossip about the canal folk. Messages were left and received, 'whip-rounds' made for bargees in distress; the sense of being one of a community was consolidated in the inn, almost the only stationary place of meeting in the canal folk's world.

The barge, rather surprisingly, evoked a folk art, one of the few to be created in the period. The low, flat-bottomed, blunt-nosed narrow boat was decorated with roses and castles in strong primary colours, red, blue, yellow and an arresting green. Roses and castles adorned water-jugs, buckets, the walls of the cabins and a framework behind the tow-horses' heads was specially made to carry the resplendent design. A comparison with gypsies again springs to the mind. Gypsies also decorate their movable homes, their caravans. They use similar bright colours but not the same motifs as the canal folk. Gypsies, however, dress themselves in a gaudy style, wearing gay scarves and head-shawls and large ear-rings dangling from their ears. In those pictures which have survived from the hey-day of canal transport, the bargees are soberly dressed and their womenfolk bundles of drab clothing —a long stuff skirt and a grey or brown woollen shawl. In one picture a couple of barefoot children are sitting with their legs over the side of the quay, watching father operate the winch.

The life, though lacking in comfort, had compensations. In spring and summer the long stretches of countryside through which the canals passed must have been very pleasant. There was not a great deal to do, except guide the tow-horse and operate the tiller. Children could run and play about the tow-path or

4.   *Child sweeping fluff* (see p. 90)

ride on the barge as they pleased. In passing through towns and at locks there was the chance of a chat with other bargees. The work was not ill-paid for the period and seems to have provided a plentiful though rough and simple diet. Perhaps one of the greatest attractions of the calling was its independence for, on the barge, the bargee was in control and free from supervision.

4

The New Machines

SHORTLY after the building of the first canal, two important machines were invented. The first, the spinning-jenny, was hand-driven. It enabled a spinner to spin a large number of threads at the same time instead of only the single thread produced by the spinning-wheel. The second machine, the water-frame, was driven by water-power. It span an even larger number of threads in less time and they were produced with much less effort by the worker. Both these machines span cotton, a textile which had been rapidly coming into use during the eighteenth century. Both machines, particularly the water-frame, were operated more economically when placed in a factory and worked by teams of people under supervision. Something of the same kind has already been described in connection with the silk industry. There were even more compelling reasons for adopting the factory system for working the jenny and the water-frame. Silk was a luxury only possible for the rich. Cotton was cheaper and could be sold in great quantities.

The capital and organization necessary to produce cotton goods for a mass market were far beyond the resources of the average domestic worker. In the last thirty years of the eighteenth century, the water-frame was adapted to spin wool and other inventions followed which were either inconvenient or impossible for domestic workshops and the factory system became established.

The spinning-jenny was invented by James Hargreaves about the year 1764. The story goes that, coming unexpectedly into the kitchen, he startled his wife so that she knocked over her spinning-wheel. As it lay on the floor, the turning wheel set him thinking of a quicker and less laborious way of spinning. He contrived a machine that could spin eight threads at a time and, in honour of his wife, he gave the machine her name, 'Jenny'. For a short time Hargreaves and his wife operated the jenny in their home, trying to keep it secret, but the neighbours soon got wind of it. Curious at first, they later became hostile for they thought that the jenny would reduce the need for spinners and so put them out of work. Poor Hargreaves was most unfortunate for not only was his house wrecked and his jenny destroyed but other men used his idea and, by improving on it, reaped most of the benefit. Within a few years jennies were spinning not eight, but eighty threads and the number was further increased to over a hundred.

Large quantities of thread were now available and this brought a period of prosperity to the weavers who were in great demand. Weavers' garrets and weaving sheds were hurriedly built in the textile districts; the price paid for weaving went up and people were eager to learn the trade. Irish immigrants thronged into Lancashire and Yorkshire and soon learnt the not too difficult craft of weaving the plainer kinds of cloth. The price of weaving doubled during the last twenty years of the eighteenth century. This was the last period in which domestic workers in wool and cotton could earn more than a bare living at their trade.

The water-frame was patented by Richard Arkwright in 1769. He was not the sole inventor for his machine embodied the previous efforts of several men. Arkwright, by assembling a number of devices and improving them produced a machine which worked effectively and could be driven by water-power. He was born in Preston in 1732, one of a large family. His father was a labourer and Richard went to work for a barber as a lather-boy when only 9 years old. He was quick and intelligent and soon learnt the job of shaving and hair-cutting. At this time, wigs were in fashion. Arkwright travelled about the country, buying the hair of village girls to use in wig-making. He experimented in dyeing hair in a wider range of colours and shades and made a little money for himself as well as increasing his master's business.

When Arkwright was 20 years of age he married a wife who had a small dowry; he moved to Bolton and set up in business as a barber and wig-maker. In

Bolton he became friendly with a clock-maker, one of the most highly skilled mechanical trades of the time. Watching his friend at work, Arkwright became interested in machinery and picked up enough knowledge and skill to start experiments on a spinning-machine. After many attempts he produced the water-frame.

In 1769, at Hockley, a small village in Lancashire, he built a factory and installed a number of his machines, using a stream as power. Water-frames required little strength or skill to operate; they could be 'minded' by quite young children. Arkwright employed children in his factory with women and men to do the more difficult work and to supervise. Thus, by combining a powered machine and the factory system Arkwright was a pioneer of modern industry. Because the power was the same as that used to grind corn in the older flour-mills, textile factories also came to be called 'mills' though the term is not strictly correct. The machinery used in the production of textiles is not a mill.

Arkwright's first factory was followed by others in the same district but, as with Hargreaves, he met great opposition from the domestic spinners who broke his windows and damaged his machines. One of his mills was completely destroyed. He moved out of Lancashire and built a large factory in a secluded valley near Cromford, Derbyshire, using the River Derwent for water-power. He brought children from the London workhouses to work his machines, housing and feeding them on the premises. The factory, which still stands, was built like a fortress round a courtyard; its massive walls had no outward-facing windows and huge bastions guarded the gates. It can be imagined that he had determined not to risk a repetition of destruction.

Arkwright made a large fortune. He improved his original machine and took out several patents. He was knighted; he became High Sheriff of Derbyshire. Towards the end of his life, he built a mansion above the banks of the Derwent from which he could look down on his now greatly extended works. Arkwright had ingenuity, ability and tenacity but he is not an attractive personality, for he was ruthless in pursuit of his aims and rode rough-shod over other people. For much of his life he was involved in lawsuits; many of his patents were challenged on the grounds that his devices had been copies. Even in an age not over-squeamish, he had the reputation of being a hard master.

Following Arkwright many other men built factories on a similar pattern. The quiet Pennine valleys were busy with the noise of machinery. The rivers of Wales and Scotland were dammed by weirs and tapped by channels, 'lades' carrying water to the great wheels which drove the machines. Other inventions, the 'mule' and the 'billy', enabled a greater variety of thread to be made. The early machines were specially designed for spinning cotton but within twenty years ways were found to spin wool by machinery driven by water-power. In 1787, the first woollen-mill was built beside the River Wharfe in Yorkshire and before the end of the eighteenth century almost all Yorkshire cloth-makers were using power in factories. The older wool-making districts of the east and south-west were slower in using the new inventions and Yorkshire rapidly outstripped them in production, becoming, as it still is, the main centre of the woollen industry.

The early textile mills, both wool and cotton, were widely scattered and their ruins can be seen in many districts such as the Lake District, East Anglia and Wales. They were thicker on the ground on the slopes of the Pennines and, as the industry developed, this concentration increased. There were many reasons but, perhaps, the most important was the character of the Pennines themselves. This hundred-mile chain has many hills with flattish tops which are covered with peat and moss. The Pennines catch the rain clouds from the Atlantic and the water is held as in a sponge. The rivers that have their source in the mosses never dry up completely because there is this reserve of water. The water is superlatively soft because of the absence of lime in the underlying rocks. Because of the heavy rainfall the climate is moist; textile fibres, particularly cotton, break less easily if worked in a damp atmosphere. The Pennine streams run swiftly from high flat tops down steep ravines, locally called 'cloughs'. These conditions are ideal for an industry requiring a continuous supply of water-power and soft water for the finishing process—bleaching, dyeing, printing and so on.

Swift streams, a consistent and plentiful water-supply, a moist climate—many of these conditions can be found in other parts of Britain but there are few where all are found to such perfection. Along many of the Pennine valleys the mills were built almost without a break. As the lower sites were occupied, mills were built high on the flanks of the hills wherever a stream could be dammed to form a head of water sufficient to turn a mill-wheel. The race for water-power was running swiftly.

Rivers, as such, are not private property but the land on their banks is, and ownership of the land carries water-rights; certain things, such as fishing, boating, using or taking water cannot be done without permission. Owners of water-rights (riparian owners) can use or lease their water-rights but the flow of water must not be hindered in a way which will harm other users of water down stream. The laws and customs which govern the use of water in rivers and streams have evolved over many centuries, mainly in connection with corn-mills. Even before the industrial revolution disputes about the various claims of the different owners were often long and bitter. As competition for water-power grew fiercer it became a publicly discussed question. The theme of two famous novels of the period centre on disputes over water-rights. In *The Mill on the Floss*, by George Eliot, a corn miller is made bankrupt and his family plunged into poverty by a prolonged lawsuit with a neighbouring miller. In *John Halifax, Gentleman,* John Halifax, a cotton spinner, is persecuted by a landowner who, in order to ruin him, withdraws water from the stream for fountains in the landowner's park.

From the 1760s to the end of the century the search for suitable sites continued. Surveyors were engaged to scour the country; advertisements appeared in newspapers offering land on the banks of rivers with, for example, 'A fall of water, 15 ft.' on the Irwell. Landowners sold or leased land with water-rights and sometimes went into business themselves. Sir George Warren was lord of the manor of Stockport, an old market town which straddles the River Mersey. Sir George owned the water-rights, an ancient corn-mill, the market and most of the land on which the town stood. He also had an overriding claim on the commons which surrounded the little town.

He sold land in and out of the town with water-rights on the Mersey and on the stream which runs into it, the Carr Brook. The purchasers built dams in a chain along both rivers and for twenty years the town was in a turmoil with disputes between Sir George and the townspeople about the interference, on so large a scale, with the water on which the town depended. The old-established corn-mill was one thing, a string of cotton-mills quite another. The corn-mill had been there for centuries; the cotton-mills were new; there were dozens of them and they used a great deal of water; they occupied land on which the townsmen claimed to have rights. The men of Stockport threatened to 'prostrate the erections' that is, pull down the mills. Nevertheless, the mills remained, increased, and became part of the landscape.

Before the industrial revolution the Warren estate was heavily mortgaged. Sir George married a Miss Jane Revell, an attractive young lady with a large fortune who chosed him from among many other men who wished to marry her. Sir George was now able to clear his estate of debt and enter into partnership with Henry Marsland, a cotton manufacturer. At this time Stockport had a ruined castle, traditionally on the site of an ancient Roman fort; Sir George levelled the ruins and built a mill for making muslins. He became a very rich man for, apart from his wife's fortune and the increasing income from his Stockport property, coal was discovered on another part of his estate. He is a good example of the way in which landowners could take part in the industrial revolution.

The mills in Stockport were in or near to an old centre of population where labour to work in them was to be had. For many mills, built in remote valleys, there were only a few scattered hamlets or farms and cottages containing but a handful of people. Even in towns, the domestic workers preferred to continue their home-crafts rather than enter the mill with regular hours and loss of independence. Another problem was that, as the new machines could be tended by children, there was little work for adults; more children were needed than could be found in a country distict at this time.

Children in Factories: The Apprentice System

The problem was solved by bringing children from other districts, mainly from the larger towns. These children were generally orphans, fatherless or motherless or without relatives able to support them. Many of them waifs who had been brought up in workhouses or in homes supported by charity. They were handed over to the mill masters under an apprentice bond, that is, the children were to work for a number of years, generally seven but sometimes five; they were to be clothed and housed and, in the later years of their apprenticeship, they sometimes received a small wage of up to a shilling a week. Their employers undertook to teach them the 'art' of cotton or woollen manufacture, though this meant little when performed on a machine. At the end of the period for which they were bound, an outfit of clothes 'suitable for their station in life' was to be provided by the employer.

The apprenticing of children was not, in the eighteenth century, a new thing. Since the days of Elizabeth I, overseers of the poor had been appointed in each parish to provide for those who could not provide for themselves, either because they were too old or too young or ill, disabled or out of work. These and other unfortunate people were given 'relief', food, clothing or money. The homeless were housed in poorhouses or workhouses and in these were many children. The children, when they were old enough to work, were found places with private families as servants, with innkeepers to help about the inns or stables or on farms as labourers. Money was sometimes bequeathed to the parish by charitable persons to apprentice destitute children so a few of the more fortunate would be bound to a master to learn a trade, such as shoemaking or carpentry. To apprentice a poor child was, therefore, to provide for him in a better way than would otherwise be his lot in life.

When the new power-driven machines created a demand for child labour on a large scale, the mill-owners applied to the overseers of the poor; the overseers were only too glad to find an opening for the children and rid the parish of a responsibility. Young children of the poorer classes had always been expected to start work at an early age; destitute children, it was thought, could hardly start too soon. Thousands of children from 6 years of age upwards were sent from London and other distant places to the textile-mills of the north. Many went from villages, from agricultural areas and some from the outskirts of the textile districts.

The village of Biddulph is on the border of Cheshire and Staffordshire. The Vicar, the Rev. James Sewel, wrote to the owner of a cotton-mill about thirty miles away asking him if he could find employment for some of the Biddulph children. The letter reads, 'The thought has occurred to me that some of the younger branches of the poor of this parish might be useful to you as apprentices. If you are in want of any of the above, we could readily furnish you with ten or more from 9 to 12 years of age of both sexes.' It is evident from the tone of this letter that the Vicar was acting from a desire to benefit the children. They were, he wrote, idle and in want.

It was not realized that conditions of apprenticeship to a craftsman for one or two children, who would share their master's home and learn a skilled trade, were very different from those in a mill. Here, the children were confined in a hot and airless factory, in attendance on machines that seldom stopped during the working day. The hours worked, generally twelve but sometimes longer, were no worse than in many other occupations but the work was monotonous—simple operations that went on and on all the time. The youngest children, small enough to crawl under the machines, swept the fluff from the floor. There was a great deal of fluff and, when collected, it was used again in the spinning process. Older children took the full bobbins off the machine and replaced them with empty ones to receive the spun thread. Others carried the full bobbins away for winding. When the thread broke on the machine it had to be tied with a special knot; young children's tiny fingers could do this well and swiftly. These and other similar operations were not hard in themselves but they became wearisome by repetition over a long day.

Sometimes the children were fed and lodged in cottages near the factory but in large mills or where there was no village near an apprentice house was provided by the employer. Some of these houses were well run, clean and with warm beds. Some were little more than sheds in which the children slept huddled together on the floor on sacks stuffed with straw, without sheets or sufficient covering. In some mills the children were well fed with a plain but varied and wholesome diet; in others all they got was bread, porridge and thin soup. Some masters were kindly and did not allow their 'overlookers' to ill-treat the children. Some were callous and brutal or indifferent and children were beaten for trivial faults and even to keep them awake at the end of a long day.

It is difficult to judge conditions in the average factory. At this time there was no check or regulation of the employer; he had almost absolute control over the way his mill was managed and over the people he employed, so all depended on the kind of person he was. The records which have come down to us relate to two extremes—the exceptionally good and the very bad employer. The records of several of the best employers enable us to see factory conditions which, though hard, were neither harsh nor cruel. For the worst employers there are two sources of evidence.

A child had the right to complain to a magistrate of wrong treatment on the part of an employer and, if the case were proved, the apprentice bond could be set aside and the child set free. Cases of this kind did occur under the older conditions of apprenticeship. A child working in a country mill and living on the premises would find it difficult to get to a magistrate even if he knew where to find one. Moreover, sometimes the magistrate was the child's employer. Very few children took this course. It is on record that cruel punishments were threatened and sometimes given to a child who complained.

Brutal treatment of factory children which resulted in death or serious bodily harm was occasionally reported to a magistrate who would then take action against the employer under common law. If the case were proved the employer would be punished. These law cases are on record. Further information about bad employers comes from the reports of inquiries into conditions under which children were employed. These reports refer to a much later period than that of the early water-power mills. The first inquiry was made in 1800, more than thirty years after the first cotton-mill was built. The following account of good and bad conditions should therefore be read bearing in mind that there were many factories, probably the majority, where conditions were in between the extremes. Of these very little is known.

Model Employers

Samuel Greg is an outstanding example of the best employers of his time. He was born in 1756; his father was a shipowner in Belfast, prosperous and well to do. Samuel was educated at Harrow and it was intended that he should go to a university and enter the Church. On leaving school he was sent to travel in Europe and, when he was in France, he visited the famous silk-mills of Lyons where water-power was used in the throwing process. He was much interested in the way water-power was used to drive machinery. He heard of the new cotton-mills recently built in England. He abandoned the idea of being a clergyman and resolved instead to build a mill and become a cotton manufacturer.

His father, who was aware of the new opportunities in this line of business, was favourable to Samuel's choice of a career and found his son some capital for the venture; for the remainder, a partner was taken. The search commenced for a suitable site—land on which to build and water to drive the machines, means of transport for raw cotton and finished goods. Clay near at hand for making bricks, stone and timber would be additional advantages to save costs in building. It was also desirable to be in or near a village. Samuel Greg appointed a surveyor to search for a site with as many of these features as possible.

After many months of disappointment the surveyor found a piece of land at Styal, on the River Bollin, in Cheshire. The site had all the advantages required except that there was no village nearer than two miles; the few inhabitants lived in scattered farms. Greg, therefore, would have to import almost all his labour force. The landowner, Sir Humphrey Trafford, was willing to sell with water-rights. The site, which Greg named Quarry Bank (because of the red sandstone outcrop on the riverside) was traversed by an ancient right of way and bridle-track which led to the Duke of Bridgewater's canal at Altrincham, about four miles away. There was also a fair road to Manchester where Greg took a house in which he lived during building operations and afterwards used as office quarters. To this house he brought a bride, Hannah Lightbody, and here his first child was born.

The mill, completed in 1785, an apprentice house for the mill children and a house for the mill manager were all built of material found on the site except for the ironwork, which was brought over the hills from Sheffield. Mill and houses are situated in a deep dell through which runs the River Bollin. The sides of the valley are thick with trees, many of them planted by Greg to replace those he cut down for building; others are ornamental or flowering trees which grace the gardens about the mill. The mill dam, which holds up the water of the Bollin to form a lake, was almost certainly built by James Brindley for, though there is no record of this, it is very similar to others that he is known to have built.

The mill is a shapely structure and is surmounted by a belfry from which a bell called the children to work from the apprentice house at the top of a small rise from the valley. The apprentice house is three stories high. It originally housed thirty children but it was enlarged from time to time to hold one hundred. The whole place is extremely attractive especially in spring and summer when the woods are full of wild flowers. The children were allowed to play in the grounds when they were not at work and on Sundays. The hours of work were from 5.30 in the morning until 8 in the evening with half an hour off for breakfast and supper and one hour for dinner—twelve and a half working time in all for six days a week—no holiday on Saturday.

On Sunday morning, the children were taken to church. They had not much time, therefore, for wandering in the woods and enjoying their lovely surroundings. Twice a day, though, they walked up and down the lane to the apprentice house and, when the machinery was being cleaned or was stopped because of a shortage of cotton or water-power, they had a free hour or so and were encouraged to go out of doors. Some of them used the opportunity to steal apples from the orchard. For this they were fined 5s. and earned the money to pay the fine by weeding the gardens and drive. Greg was a kindly man and took a great interest in the children. On his tours of inspection round the mill, he would leave 'a bright new penny' on the machine for a specially diligent and well-behaved child.

As well as stout working-clothes he provided an

attractive outfit for Sundays. On working days the girls wore light straw bonnets, tied over the head with a green ribbon, a grey dress with a large handkerchief crossed over the chest, woollen stockings, stout shoes and a grey cloak. For Sundays they had green frocks and bonnets decorated with flowers and ribbons. The boys, for work, wore dark corded breeches, stout thick jackets and 'high-crowned hats'. For Sundays they had green suits with red collars and cuffs. On the way to church, which was two miles away, both boys and girls went in procession to their employer's where Mrs. Greg and her daughters inspected them for cleanliness and neatness and gave each child a 'nosegay' (a small bunch of flowers to pin on a coat or carry in the hand).

The house built by Greg for himself and his family is next door to the mill. He had intended to continue to live in Manchester and run the mill with a manager but he had difficulty in finding a suitable man for the job—few men had either experience or training for factory management at this time. For a while he managed the mill himself and, when a manager was eventually found, Greg had become so interested in the business and in his work-people that he decided to live in Styal. All his family took part in building and running the new community. His sons entered the business and extended it; his daughters taught the boys and girls to read and write and the girls to sew; his wife saw to their health and welfare. As the business prospered, more children were employed. A school was built and a schoolmaster paid to teach the children. Later, there was even a visiting singing master.

Every child, on being apprenticed, was examined by a doctor. Greg would not take children who were not in good health or without intelligence, though this sometimes happened in spite of his and the doctor's care. Sarah Powell, a child from Liverpool, aged 9, was kept for a month before being apprenticed. The doctor reported that she had 'inflamed eyes but they are better now and there does not seem to be any objection to engaging her'. Of Clara Harrison, aged 10, the doctor wrote, 'She has enlarged glands and had better not be engaged at present.' After a time Clara was apprenticed but later her glands became worse and it was found that the unfortunate child had tuberculosis or 'consumption' as the disease was then called.

The doctor was called in to see the children when they were ill. From his reports the children seem to have been reasonably healthy and most of their ailments were the usual ones of childhood or stomach troubles. They were well fed according to the fashion of the time but, especially in winter, they were short of fresh fruit or salad. In spring they had plenty of rhubarb pudding and in autumn apple puddings and pies. Senna and arrowroot were common medicines; poultices of bread, vinegar and mustard were applied to the chest for coughs and were also used for sprains.

The children slept in dormitories, two to a bed. They rose at 5 a.m., went to the pump across the yard and washed. They then had bread and milk in the house and clattered down the hill to the mill as the bell rang for half past five.

Here they worked until 12, having porridge and milk at their work in the course of the morning. For dinner, at the apprentice house, they had beef, mutton, pork or bacon with vegetables, followed by suet pudding or fruit pie. Back in the mill at 1 o'clock, they worked until 8, with bread and milk in the afternoon. For supper they had bread and cheese or porridge; bed followed almost immediately. Particular care was taken that each child had as much food as could be eaten—there was no stint.

In the early years this diet cost Greg 3s. 6d. a week for each child. The sum would buy much more then than it does now. In later years Greg spent more on the children, partly because the cost of living went up but also because, as he grew older and richer, his natural kindliness and pride in the well-being of his apprentices increased. Towards the end of his life, the cost of keeping his apprentices was more than the wages earned by other children who lived at home. This caused some talk in the surrounding villages and it was said that the 'workhouse brats' were better off than 'free' children. Greg improved conditions for the children in other ways. For example, they were allowed time off in the evenings to attend school; he ceased to employ very young children and did not engage any whose homes were too far away for friends or relations to visit them.

At first Greg aimed at nine years as being a suitable age at which to apprentice a child though children as young as six were occasionally taken. Later, ten became the minimum and, later still, twelve. At first the children came from Liverpool, the Potteries, Birmingham and other distant towns and counties. As few of the children or their relatives, if they had any, could read or write it was difficult for them to keep in touch with each other by letter. It was even more difficult to make a long journey to visit the child at Styal. Greg's clerk would occasionally write or answer a letter from a relative. For this the child was charged with the cost of postage. Greg realized the disadvantages of complete separation and the distress it caused. As new children were required, he applied to near-by parishes. By the early nineteenth century apprentice children were seldom brought from districts more than thirty miles from Styal. Many children had no known relatives but there was often an aunt or a cousin who would take an interest in a child and visit it occasionally.

The majority of the children settled down to their new life fairly well; for many perhaps all, it was an improvement on anything they had known before. A certain number, however, found it unbearable and ran away. They were searched for, brought back and punished by fines, which they had to 'work off' by pumping water, carrying wood, gathering thistles or weeding. Undeterred, some of them ran away repeatedly. One child, Catherine Quigley, ran away twenty-five times and once was not found for two weeks. She was fined 1s. 6d. for each day she was absent. When she was brought back she sat on the steps of the mill and screamed. Catherine was exceptional; most of the truants wandered about for a few hours and were glad to return at night-fall.

The apprentice system at Greg's mill lasted for sixty years. It was at its height between 1800–20. Then, as Greg grew older and his son took charge, fewer and fewer children were taken to replace those who had worked their term of years. Samuel Greg died in 1834 and soon after his death this way of obtaining labour ceased. Nearly two thousand children had lived in the apprentice house, grown up at Quarry Bank and earned their living in the mill. Some, it is not known how many, had died. Some moved away to other jobs in other districts when they had served their time. Many continued to work at the mill as 'free labour'; they married and their children followed their example. A descendant of one of these is still living at Quarry Bank (1965).

New Communities

Even when the mill was first built work-people other than the apprentice children were employed. The proportion was small but it grew larger. As the machinery became more complicated and especially after a steam-engine was introduced to supply extra power, more men and women were needed. The mill premises were extended, for Greg's business was expanding and a larger labour force was necessary. There were only a few people in the immediate neighbourhood. Greg tried to get labourers from the surrounding villages but he found it impossible to pursuade enough to enter the mill. At this time, the 1790s, there was plenty of work for them to do at home. Those who did consent to work at Quarry Bank had at least a two-mile walk to and from the mill after a twelve-hour day, so it is not surprising to read that they 'were not available for over-time'. Greg decided to import families and provide accommodation near the mill.

For this purpose he bought land above the valley on which stood a farm-house, several barns and an old half-timbered cottage. He converted the buildings into eleven dwellings, divided the farm-house into five and the cottage into two separate houses. Here he installed the first of the imported families. They came from many parts of England but mainly from the agricultural districts of the south. They were brought with their possessions—beds, household goods and a few sticks of furniture—by canal to Altrincham and by wagon along the bridle road to Styal. This small industrial village was named Farm Fold. It was the beginning of a community of over five hundred people for Greg added to it by building rows of new houses, three stories high, in each of which lived three families.

All the work of building was done by Greg's work-people and with materials found on the spot. Even the iron-work was done by Greg's blacksmiths. The apprentice children helped on light evenings or when the machines were stopped. They were paid a few pence and no doubt enjoyed the change of work in the open air.

The incoming families came north because they were unable to find work in the agricultural districts. The population of Britain was increasing rapidly and there were more 'hands' than agriculture could employ. The overseers of the poor encouraged the out-of-work parishioners to migrate to industrial districts for otherwise they would have to be supported by the parish. Greg engaged them as a family unit, making a bargain with the father for the labour of the whole family. John Stevens, for example, was paid 26s. a week for himself, his wife and four children; John Howett had a wife and three children; he was paid 24s. There were a few fatherless families; the bargain was then made with the mother. Hannah Veasey was paid 20s. for herself and five children.

In course of time Greg enlarged Farm Fold still further by building better houses for his office staff, mechanics and foremen. Many of these had been apprentice children who had shown ability and intelligence. They had been trained as clerks, millwrights, blacksmiths, woodworkers and so on for Greg aimed at making the community at Styal as self-sufficient as possible. An outstanding example is

James Henshall who, 'By close study became an excellent accountant and arithmetician' and rose to be manager. It was at Farm Fold that the school was built. The children from the families who had settled at Farm Fold attended school until they were old enough to work. Children and adults at work attended school in the evening and on Sunday.

The Greg family were Nonconformist in religion. The apprentice children were taken to St. Bartholomew's in Wilmslow, for the Act of Parliament (1801) required that they should attend the Church of England and this was the nearest church. For their own worship and for those of their work-people who wished to attend, Greg built an Independent Church at Northcliffe, across a field from Farm Fold. Many of the work-people were, however, Methodists, for this sect made a great appeal to the new industrial working class. The Methodists were allowed to use an old wagon shed at Farm Fold and, later, Greg had a chapel built for them, finding much of the money himself.

Round these institutions, church, chapel and school, a number of clubs and societies were formed for recreation, education, and entertainment such as the Mutual Improvement Society and a choir. A small library was collected and books from the Mechanics' Institute at Wilmslow were on loan. A sick and burial club provided weekly payments or a lump sum in times of distress. Greg founded and encouraged the club for he thought that it helped his workpeople to form saving habits. Thrift was a virtue much in favour during the industrial revolution. Greg deducted the weekly payments to the club from the workers' wages.

A shop was opened at Farm Fold. This was a great boon for the two-mile trek to Wilmslow laden with groceries on the return journey was wearying and time-consuming. The shop belonged to Greg and was run by a manager. A great variety of goods was sold, many of them produced on the farmland surrounding Farm Fold which Greg had purchased when he built the village. The shop was opened in 1823, ten years before Greg died and the list of sales show an increasing improvement in the standard of living. Meat and groceries, clothes and simple furniture such as deal tables and chairs, bed-covers and hearth-rugs were on sale and so also were silk handkerchieves and scarves, ribbons for trimming Sunday bonnets, 'neckerchieves' for the men, clogs, shawls, stuff skirts and fustian trousers for everyday use.

Many people visited Quarry Bank and the settlement at Farm Fold for Greg was proud of his achievement and was glad to show visitors what he had done. Some of them left glowing accounts of the life of the community to which, especially after the early years, some comforts and graces had been added. The long hours of work, Greg's power and control over his workers both in the mill and in their homes passed without comment. The fortune that had come to him from the labour of little children aroused nothing but admiration. Most men at this time would see nothing at Quarry Bank that could be improved.

This can be seen in an account written by John Morley. 'The Gregs usually had about a hundred boys and girls between ten and twenty years and the care of them was the preoccupation of the family. They came from the refuse of the towns, yet the wise and gentle rule for the young . . . ended in the transformation of these half-starved dazed creatures who entered the gates of the factory into the best types of workpeople to be found in the district.'

The records of several other mill-owners have come down to us which show conditions like those at Quarry Bank. Samuel Oldknow, who had business dealings with Greg, built a mill and established a community at Mellor. There was a friendly rivalry between the two. Samuel Oldknow's children had, it seems, a rather more varied diet and, in the dinner hour, they were lined up for physical exercises in the mill-yard or taken into the surrounding fields for play. Samuel Oldknow was a member of the Church of England. He accompanied his apprentices across the valley to Marple Church, walking at the head of the 'crocodile'. In the church, he occupied a large square pew; the children sat in a gallery especially made for them.

Oldknow built his factory in the valley of the River Goyt which here forms the boundary between Marple and Mellor. Each district contained a village, several hamlets and many small scattered farms. Many of the inhabitants were domestic spinners and weavers. At first they were reluctant to work in Old-know's mill and, as at Styal, apprentice children were imported, in this instance, mainly from London. Later, hand-spinning became unprofitable in competition with power-spinning. Spinning was the work of women and children. No longer able to make a living, they went to work at the mill.

As we have seen, the abundance of thread produced on spinning machines found extra work for the weavers. Oldknow's mill brought a burst of prosperity to Mellor and Marple. William Radcliffe, a Mellor weaver, described how barns and outhouses were made into weaving-sheds and windows knocked into top stories to make weaving garrets. The weaver sported a gold watch on Sundays and went to church in a 'broadcloth' suit, accompanied by his wife in a silk dress. He could, so Radcliffe wrote, earn 30s. a week, a very good wage for the period. The pattern of domestic life, however, had altered: the women and children worked in Oldknow's factory; the men worked on their looms at home.

Oldknow was one of the first men in England to make muslin, a fine cotton material previously made in India. It was in great demand for ladies' dresses, cravats and ruffles for gentlemen and for fancy handkerchieves. Oldknow had an artistic turn of mind. His muslins were beautifully embroidered and decorated. The weavers who were already in the district were trained to do this specialized work and other weavers were imported. Oldknow built a number of houses for them in Marple and Mellor with special accommodation for the looms, but, unlike Greg, he was not entirely dependent on migrant labour. Marple and Mellor were established communities before Oldknow built his mill.

Oldknow was versatile and enterprising, perhaps too much so for he overspent and was often in financial difficulties. He had not sufficient capital for the many schemes he put in hand and had to borrow. To bring the River Goyt more conveniently to the site of his mill, he altered its course, constructing an elaborate system of channels and a dam large enough for boating. His buildings were made of stone, finely worked by skilful masons and handsomely decorated. He promoted the construction of a canal, the Peak Forest, which ran from the border of the limestone district of Derbyshire passed through his land at Marple and continued to Manchester. Oldknow built lime-kilns for burning lime, used it to improve his land and also sold it to farmers and to builders for making mortar or cement. He lived in a mansion called 'The Garden House' a little downstream from his mill; up on the hillside he had a stone bench placed where he could sit and gaze on his property—farmhouses and land, cottages, mill and the river turning his wheel. The bench is called 'Oldknow's Seat'.

Oldknow proposed marriage to several young ladies without success. His financial position was not secure and the ladies were advised against him by their parents. In middle life he became warmly attached to an invalid lady who had a house and estate in Marple. They did not marry but Oldknow regularly visited her and they were on terms of close friendship. His portrait hung in her room and was, it is said, specially painted for her. Towards the end of his life, Oldknow's chief creditor, Richard Arkwright (son of the promoter of the water-frame) took over the mill at Mellor and other property to pay Oldknow's debts. Oldknow remained in the business as manager. He died at Garden House and the memory of the tall, portly and kindly gentleman still lingers in the district. A millstone, carved with his initials and a spindle lies in Marple recreation ground.

The Struggle for Legal Protection

Greg and Oldknow were 'model' employers according to the low standards of their day. They did not see any reason why laws should be passed to compel other employers to treat their work-people well for this, to them, would be an interference with personal liberty. They bitterly resented any suggestion that conditions in their own mills should be under any kind of public control. Indeed, in 1800, Greg actively opposed the passing of the first Act of Parliament which restricted the hours of work for apprenticed children in cotton-mills. He went to London and interviewed M.P.s, persuading them to vote against the proposed Act.

There were, however, other cotton manufacturers

who treated their own workpeople as well or better than Greg and Oldknow who also fought long and hard for the passing of laws which would compel employers to shorten hours and improve conditions. They saw that work-people, particularly the young, left without legal protection were helpless in the hands of brutal, cruel or indifferent masters. John Fielden, of Todmorden, Robert Owen, of Lanark and Robert Peel, of Ramsbotham were outstanding in the struggle to get legal protection for child workers. Fielden and Owen both provided good conditions and worked their child-labour for shorter hours than Greg.

At Lanark, Robert Owen built a village for the mill-workers on progressive and enlightened lines and taught the advantages of co-operation between master and workers. He was successful as a cotton manufacturer and made a fortune but he was troubled by the bad effects on human beings of an industrial system which regarded labour as a source of profit only. He believed that the profits of industry belonged to all those who had produced them and that the best way to ensure this was the common ownership of the means of production. He has been called, 'the Father of British Socialism'. He spent much of his life and fortune in trying to persuade the people of Britain to his view. He did not succeed. He was, though, successful to some extent in creating a public opinion which gradually accepted the principle of legal protection in industry for the working class.

Robert Peel's ancestors were small farmers in the

Pennine country. His father had established a water-power mill on the River Irwell about fifteen miles upstream from Manchester. The mill had prospered; Robert succeeded his father in the business but, as he was well-to-do, well educated and public-spirited, he was elected M.P. for his home county and so spent a good deal of time in London. Peel's mill was unhealthy. There were several outbreaks of typhoid and other infectious diseases. The mill children were overworked and harshly treated but this Peel did not know for some time, for he left the running of the mill to a manager and 'over-lookers'. Noticing, on one of his infrequent visits, that the children looked pale and listless he made inquiries as to the cause.

He found that the manager and foremen, whose wages were based on the amount of thread produced, often drove the children too hard and too long. The children were beaten to keep them from falling asleep at the machines or offered 'some trifling bribe' to work longer. Peel consulted Dr. Percival of Manchester about the poor condition and the stunted growth of his child workers. Dr. Percival had long been concerned at the ill-health of factory children and, in 1784, had persuaded the Manchester magistrates to refuse consent to the apprenticing of children where they would be worked at night or for more than ten hours a day. Percival told Peel that he was convinced that long hours indoors and night-work were particularly harmful for children and that they should have time to play in the open air.

Peel was inclined to agree for he had noticed that the children of his farm-labourers were lively and had colour in their cheeks although they worked as hard and were not as well fed as Peel's mill children. It seems strange that this was not generally realized but little was known, at this time, of the causes of ill-health and weakness. Peel was a humane and honest man. He made a public statement of his grief at the suffering his negligence had caused; he improved conditions in his own mill; he set vigorously to work to promote a law which would protect apprentice children in general.

Aided by Owen and Fielden and by other public-spirited and humane men, Peel's Act was passed in 1801. It was the first act to regulate the new conditions of factory work created by the industrial revolution. The Act only applied to parish apprentices who worked in cotton- or woollen-mills. Children were not to work more than twelve hours a day and they were not to work at night between the hours of 9 p.m. and 6 a.m. The premises were to be kept clean and airy. Boys and girls must sleep in separate rooms and not more than two in a bed. They were to be taught reading, writing and arithmetic and must be allowed time off for this purpose and they must be given religious instruction. The Act, therefore, did not go very far in improving the children's plight but it had far-reaching effects.

The passing of the Act and the public discussion in connection with it aroused the conscience of many people who had not previously been aware of the evils connected with the employment of children in factories. Moreover, because the law was not generally obeyed, for no adequate provision had been made to enforce it, Peel, Owen and Fielden now had a larger body of interested and determined people with them to press for stronger measures. Also, it was seen that 'free-labour children'—those who lived with their parents, should be protected. In 1816 a committee of inquiry was set up with Robert Peel as chairman. Many different people, including some employers, gave evidence. The findings of the committee were published and it is plain that in the majority of factories conditions were totally unsuitable and bore hardly on children, while in some factories conditions were shockingly callous and brutal.

Harsh Employers and Bad Conditions

Ainsworth, Catterall and Company employed about 150 parish apprentices in their cotton-mill at Backbarrow, a thinly populated district at the southern end of Lake Windermere. The mill was situated on a river which runs into Morecambe Bay. Children had been brought to this remote and lonely place from London, 300 miles away. A few had been brought from Liverpool. Some of them were only 7 years old; others ranged from 8 to 15 years. All were bound apprentice until they were 21. They worked normally from 5 a.m. till 8 p.m. with one hour off for dinner for a six-day week; they cleaned the machines on Sunday morning. When there was pressure of work, the hours were from 5 a.m. till 9 or 10 p.m. and they sometimes worked these hours continuously for three weeks. They slept on the floor with a rough blanket over and under them and the blanket was never washed.

At a time previous to the inquiry, the proprietors of the mill had been in financial difficulties owing to shortage of orders. The mill was closed for a time and the children were, in the overlooker's words, 'set at liberty, not forced to go'. They were taken in a cart and turned adrift on the sands of Morecambe Bay. When questioned about the condition of the children, the overlooker said, 'To be sure they would not be well off; they would have to beg their way or something of that sort.'

Theodore Price, a magistrate, gave evidence concerning a mill near Warwick. He had found the atmosphere in the workrooms 'very close' and thick with 'downy parts that blew off the cotton'. The children breathed air laden with these particles and 'were given emetics to make them vomit it back'. He asked if the windows could not be opened and was told that this would only make it worse for the wind would blow the fluff about. Price reported, 'I thought the children short in stature and they had a hectic (flushed) appearance. There was a moisture about their faces.' They worked thirteen hours a day with one hour break for dinner. Other food was eaten 'at their work, for to put the mill out of gear for a stopage' was time-wasting. 'It took a long time to put it back.'

The children were not brutally treated at Emscott mill and they were allowed to play along the banks of the river when they were not at work. Their lodging-house was near to the mill. Price was asked about the morals and behaviour of the child apprentices. He thought they had little opportunity to be ill-behaved and that 'no crime such as theft was possible as the children could not go off the premises. They appeared as complete prisoners as they would be in gaol'. Their beds and the house were 'clean and comfortable. All that struck me and afflicted my mind was their want of recreation, their solitude and unvarying scenes'. There were forty children in this mill.

An employer from Congleton, Cheshire, thought that loss of freedom was good for the children. He compared his apprentices to 'free labour' children. 'They are so far favourable that it (confinement in a factory) keeps them out of mischief. They are less likely to contract evil habits than if they are idling away their time.' This employer, when asked at what age he took apprentices said, 'Generally about seven. I really am not in the habit of asking their ages. I suffer the little ones not to come before breakfast.' That is, between 7 and 8 o'clock. Even so, they would work at least ten hours.

It was generally agreed that cotton factories were more unhealthy than those in which silk was manufactured. It was not necessary to keep the workrooms hot and moist and silk waste did not fly about to the same extent. A silk manufacturer from Bruton, Somerset, said that he kept the rooms at a comfortable temperature, not too hot and not too cold. He provided stools for the children to sit on when the work allowed, not at all the usual practice. He took the children as early as 6 years. The evidence of many more witnesses could be given but these examples are enough to show how urgent was the need for reform, supervision and control.

As to the fate of the individual child apprentice, little can be seen from the report of 1816. The children themselves were not asked to give evidence. An inquiry was made into the whereabouts of 2,026 parish apprentices who had been sent from London. It was found that 438 could not satisfactorily be accounted for; 80 were known to be dead; 166 had run away; 26 were in workhouses and 18 were incapable of work. The remainder were still at work or in the army or navy.

The words of one child apprentice from this period have come down to us. Bridget Earnshaw was born in 1800. When she was an old lady of 86 years, she recalled her experiences as a parish apprentice to the master of a small factory in Stockport and her story was published in the local paper, the *Stockport Advertiser:*

My father died when I was very young. When I was ten years old I was taken to Stoppord Moor to be apprenticed to a small weaver or manufacturer. There was another apprentice besides myself but she was just out of her time. . . . We had oatmeal porridge, skimmed milk and oat cakes for breakfast, potatoes and buttermilk with occasionally a little bacon for dinner and porridge for supper. We had no beer, tea, new milk nor butcher's meat and no change on Sunday. My master had a terrible instrument called a twig whip, made from a number of long taper twigs plaited together, so that it was thick at one end and ended in a single thin twig at the other. If I looked away from my work he would beat me with this whip. He would not speak, but he would often beat me with little or no reason. He was equally cruel with his own children. His wife was a kind-hearted woman but dared not interfere and even his brother would not speak to him. On one occasion he told me to tie a weaver's knot and because I did not draw it tight he beat me till I was bruised all over my body. At last I could endure it no longer and ran away but I was caught and suffered a worse beating than any previous one. He seized me by the hair and threw me against the loom, bruising my head and blacking my eyes.

The neighbours complained at the treatment of the unfortunate child and Bridget was taken from the factory on Stockport Moor and sent to a hand-loom weaver who employed a few women and children. Bridget was 11 and this time she was not apprenticed. Her wages were 2s. a week: she paid 1s. for lodging and '1s. for my porridge'. Like many aged people, Bridget's memory of her childhood was strong and vivid. She remembered the details of the whip with great particularity.

As a result of the report made by the committee of inquiry an Act of Parliament was passed in 1819 which gave apprentice children a little more protection. They were not to be sent more than forty miles from their home parish; they were not to be employed at an earlier age than 9 years; children under 16 were not to work at night or for more than twelve hours a day. These regulations also applied to 'free-labour' children. The Act only applied to children in cotton factories. Several other Acts were passed within the next twenty years but still the law was not generally obeyed.

Free-labour Children

In 1833, over fifty years after the system of employing children in factories had been established, an important Act gave real and substantial protection by appointing paid inspectors and providing penalties where the law was not observed. Great changes had happened in these fifty years. The growing use of steam instead of water-power was causing the textile industry to be moved from rural districts into towns in or near the coal-fields. Here children of families in the locality could be employed in mills. The reluctance and distaste for factory work was slowly broken down as the domestic industries one by one were replaced by machines and the factory system. We have seen how the spinners could not earn a living wage by hand-spinning in competition with the water-frame. After about 1800, a power-loom, invented by Edmund Cartwright, a clergyman, came into general use. Domestic hand-loom weavers earned less and less for a week's work. The 30s. of the hand-loom weavers' 'hey-day' fell to 10s. and, by 1830, only 6s. could be earned in a seven-day week, working twelve hours a day.

To help out the family income, the children went into the factories. Hand-loom weaving persisted for a surprisingly long time; in silk until the end of the nineteenth century and for special work, even into the present century. In the cotton and wool industries an increasing number of adults joined their children in factory employment until, in the textile districts, the life of the family was dependent on the mill.

Public opinion, at this time, was against any legal regulation or control of working conditions for adults. It was thought that they should make their own individual bargains with their employers. There was, however, a growing sense of the need for the protection of 'free labour' children and we have seen that a start had been made by the Act of 1819. By 1830 the 'free-labour' children greatly outnumbered the parish apprentices. In textiles, the factory system now employed over a quarter of a million people. Of these 56,000 were children under 13 years of age;

108,000 were 'young persons' between the ages of 13 and 18.

The struggle to obtain legal protection for 'free labour' children and 'young persons' which would improve conditions and shorten hours was long and hotly contested. Two men were outstanding on the children's behalf—Lord Shaftesbury and Michael Sadler. The plight of children in the woollen industry was championed by Richard Oastler. They and many others who also took a leading part in the agitation were supported by a large and growing body of men from all religious sects and all political parties. Working men and women had given some support to the earlier measures but the weakness of their organizations and their poverty had prevented their efforts from being much regarded. In the campaign for the Factory Act of 1833, they presented petition after petition, helped to prepare evidence and supported the many hundreds of meetings held to create a public opinion sufficiently strong to pass the measure. The adult workers hoped for legal protection for themselves as well as for children but in this they were disappointed.

The three men who led the campaign, Shaftesbury, Sadler and Oastler, were very different in outlook, disposition and social class. Shaftesbury, the youngest of the three, was in his late twenties. He was heir to a large landed estate in Dorset. Until his father's death, his title was Lord Ashley but, to avoid confusion, in this book he will be called Shaftesbury throughout.

He had been educated at Harrow and Christ Church, Oxford. The Duke of Marlborough was his uncle. At 26 years of age he was elected M.P. for Wood-stock, the parliamentary division in which the Duke had a controlling influence.

Shaftesbury was a deeply religious man, acutely sensitive and soon thrown into self-doubt and depression by criticism. Yet his life was spent in urging and promoting reforms of the kind which provoked bitter hostility and personal attacks from his opponents and from members of his own social class. His father neither understood nor sympathized with him or his aims. The relationship between them became strained and, finally, broken. One result of the unhappy breach was that, while his father lived, Shaftesbury was often very short of money for his allowance was purposely kept extremely small.

Shaftesbury was not politically progressive. His motives in trying to better the lot of the poor and helpless were those of humanity, pity and mercy. He was deeply grieved when he found that these motives did not lead others to action. 'I first began in hope', he said, 'that many of the aristocracy would first follow me and then succeed me. Not one is to be found; a few, at my request, put their hands to the plough but they looked back and returned not to the furrows.' This is an exaggeration; many landed gentlemen supported reforms of various kinds though not with the patient persistence of Shaftesbury. His feeling of isolation and loneliness was partly due to his inability to make warm and friendly contacts. He was not 'good with people'. Even the oppressed and wretched, whose lot in life was relieved by Shaftesbury's lifelong efforts, misunderstood and distrusted him.

In contrast to the strife and disillusion of Shaftesbury's public life and his miserable relationship with his father, his marriage was happy and successful. His wife was a beautiful and charming woman who shared his concern for the poor and helpless. It was she who influenced him to take up the cause of the factory children. Their plight was brought to his notice by Michael Sadler. Michael Sadler was born in 1780. He was an early Methodist and, in his youth, was active in assisting the spread of Methodism in Yorkshire. He was a merchant in Leeds, importing Irish linens. Thus he came into contact with industry without being, himself, a manufacturer and was able to see conditions of labour with a clearer eye than if he had been an employer.

Sadler took an enthusiastic interest in politics. In 1829 he was elected Tory M.P. for Newark, Nottinghamshire. During the years 1831–2 when the agitation for factory reform was gathering strength, he was M.P. for Aldborough, Yorkshire. His connection with Ireland led him to investigate the problems of that unhappy country and he wrote a book, *Ireland; its Evils and their Remedies*. He had an independent mind as well as a kind and humane disposition. He, like Robert Owen, opposed the generally held view that problems connected with labour should be judged from the standpoint of profit-making.

Human happiness and dignity were, he held, more important and if profits could not be made without these being sacrificed, then so much the worse for profits. It was this attitude that endeared him to the mill-workers. He became the representative in Parliament of the committees set up in the textile districts to secure a ten-hour day. He brought a Bill before the House of Commons for, among other reforms, a ten-hour day for factory workers. The House decided that more evidence was necessary of the hardships of long hours of work. John Fielden who, you will remember, supported the Apprentice Act of 1801 and who was M.P. for Oldham, expressed himself in forthright style. He could not imagine why anybody wanted evidence to be convinced that children of 10 years of age were not fit to work for twelve hours a day. Many other M.P.s urged the passing of the Bill but there was strong pressure from the textile manufacturers. They said that they would be ruined as industry could not work profitably without the labour of children. It was, they argued, in the last hours of the twelve that profit was made. The previous hours paid the cost of production.

John Fielden and his brother owned one of the largest textile businesses in England. Their factory workers already had as good conditions and the same hours as those proposed in the Bill. Far from being ruined, the Fieldens had made a fortune. Fielden wrote a pamphlet, *The Curse of the Factory System*, in which he exposed the evils of overwork and bad conditions. Nevertheless, the House of Commons was not convinced, the passage of the Bill was adjourned and a committee of inquiry into the condition of children in factories was appointed with Michael Sadler as chairman.

Sadler's practical mind moved him to action of a new and startling kind. Under his chairmanship the men, women and children from the factories were brought before the committee of inquiry and, in their own homely language, told the tale of their suffering and hardship. The conscience of the British people was shocked and there was a public outcry on a much larger scale than had previously been aroused on this issue. Petitions, resolutions from meetings, letters and articles in the newspapers, deputations from a variety of organizations and a growing body of protest from the factory workers made it impossible for the government not to take action. Unfortunately, Sadler lost his seat at the general election of 1832 and the cause of the factory workers lost its leader in Parliament.

After some consideration the delegates from Lancashire and Yorkshire chose Lord Shaftesbury. He had not previously interested himself in the movement for factory reform but he was known to have a heart and conscience for the sufferings of the oppressed. As the heir to a landed estate he had

the prestige of his position. He was young and energetic. When Sadler lost his seat in the House of Commons, Shaftesbury had written to him offering his
services but with no thought of the leadership. 'I
can perfectly recollect my astonishment, doubt and
terror at the proposition', he wrote and asked for
time to consider the matter. After talking it over
with his wife and 'after meditation and prayer' he
agreed to be the spokesman of the factory workers
and present the Ten Hour Bill to the House of Commons.

For some time there had been a few organizations
in the textile districts whose aim had been the en-
forcement of the laws passed in 1801 and 1819. New
organizations, called Short-time Committees were
formed in rapidly increasing numbers to support the
Ten Hour Bill. Two central committees were formed,
one in Manchester and one in Bradford. It was from
these central committees that the local members were
kept in touch with what was happening in London.
Shaftesbury was recommended to the Short-Time
Committees as 'noble, benevolent and resolute in
mind as he is manly in person'.

Many of the factory workers, perhaps the majority,
could not read or write. They spoke the broad dialect
of Lancashire and Yorkshire. They were not used to
public speaking and were unskilled in debate though
they were, by experience, learning to organize. Not
many of the national leaders of the various move-
ments for reform were drawn from the working

people, their main function was to provide mass membership of the local organizations. They supplied the weight behind the national leaders.

John Doherty, the secretary of the Cotton Spinners' Union, was an outstanding exception; he was not only clear-sighted and intelligent but could also express himself with eloquence and punch. He wished the workers to be protected from low wages and long hours, but he also fought for them to be represented in Parliament so that they could have a hand in making the laws that govern the nation, working men and employers alike. Doherty suffered three years' imprisonment for expressing these opinions. The movement for the Ten Hour Bill threw up numbers of local leaders but, apart from Doherty, the national leaders were men of social standing.

The leader in Yorkshire was a land agent, Richard Oastler. He was a tall, red-headed, forthright Yorkshireman with a fiery temper and a burning hatred of injustice and oppression, which he expressed in strong and sometimes outrageous language. He had been trained as an architect and, when he was 32 years of age, he became steward to an estate near Huddersfield in the West Riding of Yorkshire. Huddersfield was in the centre of the wool-manufacturing district. The development of the cotton industry and the evils connected with it were repeated here, though a little later in time. Oastler had been active in the campaign for the abolition of slavery in British dominions and, when this was achieved in 1833, he turned his attention to the employment of children in factories. He was then about 40 years old.

Oastler opened a national campaign for the Ten Hour Bill by writing a series of letters to the newspapers on 'Yorkshire Slavery' which he declared to be as bad as anything to be found overseas on cotton plantations. A West Indian slave-owner, on hearing of the hours worked in woollen-mills had said to Oastler, 'I have always thought myself disgraced by being the owner of slaves but we never thought it possible for any human being to be so cruel as to require a child of 9 years old to work twelve and a half hours a day and that, you acknowledge, is your regular practice.' During the campaign for freeing slaves, Oastler had worked with many mill-owners. He taunted and jibed at them for not being equally anxious to free their own 'slaves'.

Oastler's 'Yorkshire Slavery' letters were followed by a series of indoor and outdoor meetings at which he and many others made fiery orations to excited crowds. The industrial districts were in a turmoil and the country generally was rent by conflicting arguments. Meanwhile, Sadler's committee of inquiry listened for forty-three days to stories of hardship, almost unbelievable misery and, in some instances, cruelty and brutality. The following examples are taken from the report issued by this committee. As the examples given in a previous section of this book refer to children in cotton-mills the examples now given are taken mainly from the woollen industry. The children tell their own stories:

'I am twelve years old. I have been in the mill for twelve months. I have worked overtime for three weeks together.' The girl was asked if she worked overtime from choice and answered, 'No, them as work must work.' She continued, 'I go to Sunday school sometimes. I mean to go regular. I want to be a scholar.' An 11-year-old told of her weariness. 'We had been working from six in the morning and Castles (the overlooker) asked us whether we were agreeable to work all night on because it was Christmas week. He wanted something for himself. (Castles was paid on production.) We were tired but he let us have a lie down in the night a little while. We went on working till 9 o'clock the next night. We were very tired then. I fell asleep the second day once or twice. Castles did not strap me for it that day.'

Parents, driven by poverty but also sometimes callous and indifferent to their children's suffering, urged the reluctant to work. 'I began work a little before I was five years old,' said William Pickles of Bradford. 'I got my knees bent with standing so long. When we tired, you know, there was nought to sit on. I was obliged to lay hold of sommat to keep me up.' William's father was a hand-loom weaver who earned about 10s. a week. His mother went out 'washing for folks'. She earned 1s. a day and her food. There were four children of whom William was the eldest. 'I have asked my father and mother to let me stop away sometimes. They said they could not do with me laiking (playing) at home, there was so many of us laiking from being not old enough (to work).'

A little boy complained to his mother of being whipped with a strap and kicked for being slow at his work. She gave him a halfpenny 'not to mind and go back to work like a good boy'. Sometimes, the child said, he would be surly and would not go. His mother would then talk about the halfpenny. Sometimes he got it and sometimes not. Ellen Hootton, near 10 years old, said that she was beaten about twice a week. When asked if it hurt much, she answered, 'No, but it made my head sore.' A shocking tale of ill-treatment was told by a witness from Scotland. When she was a child 'too little to put my ain clothes on', the overlooker used to beat her 'till I screamed again. The boys were beat till they fell to the floor in the course of the beating.'

Sadler did not spare himself in his efforts to make the plight of the children known and as a result his health suffered. Shortly after losing his seat in Parliament at the election of 1832, he became seriously ill. He died in 1835. As we have seen, the children's cause in the House of Commons was taken up by Shaftesbury. In 1833, he reintroduced Sadler's Bill. Although there was considerable approval for the measure, its passage was further delayed by the appointment of yet another committee of inquiry.

It would be wearisome and, in this book, unnecessary to follow the progress and report of this committee in any detail. The committee's representatives had a hostile reception in the textile areas for it was felt, with truth, that they had been appointed with the intention of discrediting the Sadler Report. In Leeds they were mobbed by children singing one of the songs of the time:

> We will have the Ten Hour Bill, that we will, that we will.
> Else the land will ne'er be still, never still, never still.
> Parliament say what they will, we shall have the Ten Hour Bill.

By this time, the case for limiting the hours worked by children had been accepted by the majority of people though reluctantly by many employers. The main difficulty now to be met was that a ten-hour day for children would be likely to mean a ten-hour day for adult workers, since the labour of adults depended on the work of children. Adult workers were hoping that this would happen but public opinion was very much against any interference with the conditions of adult labour. A compromise was proposed and the Factory Act (1833), sponsored by Lord Shaftesbury, passed into law.

The Act applied to all textile mills. In order not to interfere with the hours for adults, children were to work in shifts of not more than eight hours a day. This was an improvement on the previous proposals. They were not to be employed at all under nine years of age. 'Young persons' between 12 and 18 were to work for twelve hours only. No one under 18 was to work at night. Two whole and eight half holidays were to be given each year. A child must have a doctor's certificate of good health before commencing work and must receive some education during the hours of labour.

Most important of all, four full-time inspectors were appointed to see that the Act was carried out. Employers could be fined for disobeying the provisions of the Act. Although it took time, conditions in factories steadily improved. Children had much more legal protection than at any previous time. Their conditions of work were not, it goes without saying, those which we would consider possible but an important and substantial improvement had been made. Sixty years and more had passed since child labour was first used in textile factories. Several generations of unprotected children had laboured in the mills.

5

The Giant, Steam

In 1769, the same year in which Arkwright patented the water-frame, James Watt patented the steam-engine. It was first used for pumping the water from mines but soon it was adapted to drive machines of many kinds. Steam-engines were installed in water-power mills to run the machines during a shortage of water; new textile-mills using steam instead of water began to be built; steam-engines were used in iron-making; in the early nineteenth century steam-ships sailed on the River Clyde, many industries, such as brewing, pot- and china-making used steam power in one or other of the processes.

An enthusiastic account of the wonders of the steam-engine, written in the early nineteenth century, claimed that the power of four million men had been added, by its aid, to the resources of Britain. Only a guess, it is nevertheless expressive of how people regarded steam. A giant had arrived and the industrial revolution gathered immense speed and force with the added weight. The invention and persever-ance of James Watt made this possible. His life will be told in some detail because it enables us to see another aspect of the industrial revolution and brings us into contact with people from many walks of life.

Many of the men who, in association with Watt, launched the steam-engine were wealthy and well educated, for to produce it on a large scale needed a great deal of money and business knowledge. To make the engine and keep it in order required more skill than was necessary for the older types of machines. The new technical knowledge gained in developing the steam-engine was the beginning of modern engineering. This can be seen happening at the workshop level and it is possible to gain some knowledge of the life of the metal-worker and mechanic. Moreover, in considering the life of James Watt we cover a large part of Great Britain, beginning in Scotland, following him to Birmingham and making journeys with him to London, Cornwall, Wales and other districts. Something, also can be learnt of the people who bought his engines and the men who worked them.

James Watt was born in 1736 at the small river port of Greenock on the Clyde. His grandfather was a teacher of mathematics and his father was a master carpenter and shipwright and also a builder, coffin-maker and general merchant. He was able to turn his hand to a variety of practical jobs. He repaired ships' instruments, he made a crane for the harbour, bought, sold and repaired pumps, made household furniture and kept a shop stocked with the kind of articles used on board ship. He was comfortably off, respected in the town and held, at one time or another, the offices of town councillor, treasurer and magistrate. His wife, James's mother, was a good-looking, good-tempered, cheerful woman who ran the house with thrift and good management. There were five children; three died in childhood and one, a lad, was drowned at sea. James was the only surviving child.

The Watts lived in a house on the riverside with a shop and workshop on a small piece of land near by. James was not strong. Perhaps because of the loss of the other children, his parents cosseted him. He did not go to school and he did not care to run about and play with other boys and girls. His mother taught him to read and his father taught him writing and arithmetic. His father gave him a set of tools and encouraged him to make toys and small articles. His mother allowed him to draw with chalk on the flags that paved the kitchen. It might have been better if his parents had encouraged him to take more exercise in the fresh air for he suffered continually from violent headaches, indigestion and biliousness in childhood and throughout his life.

As a consequence, he was seldom cheerful, tended to look on the black side of things and was often miserable. Nevertheless he had a good temper and disposition, was gentle, affectionate and inoffensive. He was a good son to his father and mother; he made lasting friendships. His most remarkable quality was perseverance for, though often in despair, he would not give up. His inventions took many years to bring to perfection and many more before they were financially successful. With dogged endurance, though not without complaint, he met and overcame endless difficulties and frustrations. His portrait shows a strong but joyless face, marked with the scars of the struggle. He found his greatest satisfaction in his workshop. Here, his mechanical genius completely absorbed him. He forgot his ill health and the difficulties that confronted him.

When James was about 14 years old he was sent to Greenock Grammar School. His frequent illnesses prevented him from attending with regularity but he made good progress, particularly in mathematics. Education in Scotland, at this time, was more widely spread than in England. As early as the seventeenth century, small-town and village schools were established by law. The science of the day was taught as well as the more usual classics. Literacy was more common and it was not unusual for people in quite humble circumstances to have a shelf of books. James's father had a good library so, when James was unable to attend school, he browsed through books on Scottish history, astronomy, mathematics and religion and also on a book of Border Ballads which he learned by heart, re-reading till the book was tattered.

He was still a quiet, studious lad, not happy in the company of those of his own age. He took long solitary walks along the banks of the Clyde and often fished in its waters, a tranquil occupation that suited him and allowed him to think out the problems of geometry and mathematics which were his main interest.

It had been intended that James should work under his father in the family business but, as James's abilities were of a more exact, mechanical and scientific quality than would be necessary in a shipwrights' yard, it was decided that he should be trained as a mathmatical instrument maker. This was a highly skilled trade requiring great precision and a good knowledge of mechanics. At 18 years of age, James went to Glasgow in search of a master who would take him as an apprentice. He took with him one small trunk containing a change of stockings and underwear, a leather apron, a set of joinery and other tools and a quadrant, 'probably of his own making'.

In 1754, when James Watt arrived in Glasgow, the city was very small: there were only two main streets. Then as now, Glasgow had a cathedral and a university. The principal trade was in tobacco, brought from America in sailing-ships which moored at the quays on the Clyde. No mathematical instrument maker was to be found so, rather than return home and burden his father, Watt went to work for a mechanic who made, among other things, spectacles, fiddles, fishing-tackle and some of the simpler instruments such as dividers and rulers. Watt's master was a handy 'Jack of all trades' but there was not much that he could teach that Watt did not already know. Fortunately, in returning some work done for the University, Watt was introduced to Professor Dick who, seeing Watt's ability, gave him some excellent advice and, later, befriended him.

In the Professor's opinion Watt should go to London and seek an apprenticeship with a competent master. So, after consulting his father, Watt sent his trunk by sea to London and set off himself on horseback. He made first for Newcastle and then rode down the Great North Road. The journey took a fortnight. He had a few pounds in his pocket and a letter of introduction from the Professor. At this time there were no stage-coaches or other public services between Glasgow and London.

The finest craftsmanship in the country was concentrated in London. There were instrument makers in plenty but the terms they offered were such that Watt could not accept. The usual seven years were too many for an 18-year-old of Watt's ability and knowledge. Also, it was not usual for craftsmen in London to take apprentices who were not sons of 'freemen of the city', that is, inhabitants with special rights. However, after much searching, Watt found a master, John Morgan, himself highly skilled, who undertook to give Watts a year's instruction for 'twenty guineas and the proceeds of his labour during that time'.

The London to which Watt came in the middle of the eighteenth century, was by far the largest town in England or, indeed, in Europe. About a million persons lived in or near the city. The population of greater London was one-tenth of the total population of England, Wales and Scotland put together. It was the centre of trade and commerce. The Thames was busy with ships from Europe, America and India; trade with China had commenced and was increasing.

London was, as now, the seat of government and the centre of fashion, culture and learning. It was a city of great contrasts, for many wealthy landowners and merchants had town houses here while not far away there were slums of appalling filth. In London there was, to a greater extent than in any other town, a large middle class. There were many skilled domestic workers who, especially in the luxury trades of silk-making and furnishing, were comfortably circum-stanced or even well-to-do. London shops drew purchasers from all over the country; in the best shops, apprentices paid a high premium and were often the younger sons of gentlemen. Fine fabrics and furniture of an excellence than has not been surpassed was made for the great country houses which were a fashion in the eighteenth century.

For amusement and recreation there were several theatres and concert halls, the Tower, which was a zoo as well as a museum, countless public houses, some with skittle alleys, trips on the Thames to pleasure gardens and many other attractions. James Watt, choking with a persistent cough in the smoke-laden air, racked with rheumatic pains and suffering from chronic indigestion, did not like London at all. He was intent on learning his job so that he could earn his living. His father's circumstances were not too prosperous. He sent money from time to time but Watt worked after hours 'till my hands were shaking' in order to earn something towards his keep and so cause his father as little expense as possible. Board and lodgings cost 8s. a week; Watt could not live on less, he wrote his father, 'without pinching my belly'.

At the end of the year he was competent in the making of scales, rulers, 'parallels', theodolites and all the instruments then in use. 'I have made', he wrote to his father, 'a brass sector with a French joint, as nice a piece of framing in the trade.' The term 'nice' was used in the sense of 'precise'. He proposed to come home for a while to recover his health and then to set up in business. His father sent him sufficient money for the purchasing of tools not easily to be found in Scotland and for the journey. He arrived home exhausted. After a short holiday at Greenock his cough ceased to trouble him though the 'sick headache' then and afterwards continued.

Watt's next move was to return to Glasgow where he tried, without success, to find suitable premises for an instrument-maker's shop with living accommodation. The craftsmen of Glasgow were as jealous of their rights as the craftsmen of London; they would not allow 'strangers' to practise a trade in the town. Dr. Dick, whose advice and help had sent Watt to

London, used his influence to provide Watt with rooms in a quadrangle in the University precincts. Here Watt lived and worked, repairing and making instruments for the professors of natural science and also making a variety of things for sale. A Glasgow newspaper of 1759 contains the following advertisement:

> Just published and to be sold by James Watt, at his shop in the college of Glasgow, Price 2/6
> A large sheet map of the River Clyde, from Glasgow to Portincross from an actual survey

The Clyde had been surveyed by Watt's uncle. Watt published and sold copies of the map.

He made musical instruments, flutes, guitars and, an order from Dr. Black, Professor of Natural Science, a barrel organ. This instrument plays a tune when a handle is turned. Dr. Black was delighted with it and Watt, emboldened by success, next made a 'finger' organ, a much more intricate piece of work. He became known to the University staff as a skilful and reliable craftsman who could turn his hand to any number of things. They often came to his room to watch him at work. With many of them, in particular, Dr. Black, Watt formed close and lasting friendships. The conversation of learned men of science and the books in the college library, which he was allowed to use, gave Watt the chance to develop his own talent as well as enlarging his mind and imagination. He remained modest and retiring in manner but became easier in meeting people.

Life in the college precincts was exceedingly congenial but a shop tucked away in a quadrangle did not attract a lot of outside custom. In order to extend his business, about the year 1760 Watt went into partnership with John Craig, who found the capital for a shop in the Trongate, one of the principal streets of Glasgow. The business prospered and in four years' time sixteen men were being employed. During this time Watt still lived in college but, in 1764, when he was 28 years old, he took and furnished a house in 'plain yet comfortable style'. To this house he brought a young wife, Margaret, his cousin.

Margaret had a lively and cheerful disposition. She saw to her husband's comfort, looked after him during his bouts of sickness and encouraged him when he was depressed. A son was born and was given the family name of James. During this time Watt seems to have been as happy as his clouded disposition allowed. His business was bringing in a moderate income, his wife relieved him of the details of daily living and he had some leisure in the quiet evenings at home to pursue his studies.

For some time past he had been interested in steam as a source of power. Several methods of using it had been tried in the previous fifty years and one type of engine, designed by Thomas Newcomen, was found to be effective in pumping water from mines, feeding water into canals and blowing furnaces. Newcomen's engine, however, had serious defects and its use was limited. Several of the professors of Glasgow University were interested in the problem and Watt had been making a series of experiments on steam pressure for them.

At the time of his marriage, Watt was engaged in repairing a Newcomen engine. In trying to correct its deficiencies he designed an improvement which led to a change in the character of the engine. Working from this point, after five years of effort and many failures he succeeded in producing an engine of a new and better type. In 1769, the Watt Steam Engine was patented. It was much cheaper in use than the Newcomen engine; in course of time improvements added technical advantages and the earlier engine became obsolete. A letter from Watt when he was nearing the crisis of invention shows his excitement and absorption in his work. 'I have now almost a certainty of the *facturum* (workability) of the fire-engine. . . . If there be not some devil in the hedge, mine ought to raise water to 44 ft. with the same quantity of steam that theirs (Newcomen's) does to 32. In short, I can think of nothing else but this machine.'

Years of invention were followed by years during which Watt struggled with the problems connected with manufacturing the engine for industrial use. To construct it required new skills and few men were to be found who could work with the precision necessary to prevent the escape of steam from the cylinders. Capital was needed and Watt had very little. He went into partnership with Dr. Roebuck, an ironmaster and mine-owner. Dr. Roebuck's mine was flooded and he hoped to be able to clear it of water by using the Watt steam-engine. Many adjustments have to be made before a model, which may work on a bench, is a practical success on the job. Before Watt had overcome the difficulties, Dr. Roebuck was financially ruined, Watt's small capital had gone and he was in debt to, among other people, his old friend, Dr. Black.

These setbacks would have discouraged a far more optimistic person than James Watt. 'Of all things in life', he wrote, 'there is nothing more foolish than inventing.' Again, speaking to a friend, 'Today I enter the 35th. year of my life and I think I have hardly yet done 35 pence worth of good in the world.' He resolved to work no more on the engine but that was an impossibility. Nevertheless, a living must be earned for the shop in the Trongate had been neglected and was making very little money.

Watt closed the shop and commenced in business as a surveyor. In this new vocation he was familiar with the instruments used for he had been making them for years; his knowledge of mathematics and geometry and his adaptable genius did the rest. He was first commissioned for small jobs, such as surveying land to settle problems of boundaries but quite soon he was tackling plans and estimates for harbours, bridges and canals.

The idea of a new method of water-transport had spread from England to Scotland. Watt surveyed a

I 119

number of canals of which the most important was the Caledonian, which connects the lochs between Inverness and so divides Scotland in half. This canal was afterwards constructed by Telford but, in some other instances, Watt acted as supervising engineer. Of the Monkland Canal he took full charge; he was surveyor, superintendent, engineer and treasurer. Not only had he to cope with the technical details; he had to hire and manage gangs of navvies, pay them their wages and haggle over piece-work. He did not like this. 'I would rather', he declared, 'face a loaded cannon than settle an account or make a bargain.' Nevertheless, like it or not, he learned how to administer and handle labour and the experience thus gained was to be exceedingly useful.

In 1773, he was working in the Highlands of Scotland, a country at that time almost without roads or towns, wild and remote. It had rained incessantly. Working in a sea of mud, discouraged at the failure to launch his invention and anxious about his wife, he received a message that she was seriously ill. A child was expected but, before Watt could reach her, both she and the child were dead. He had lost, as he said, the comfort of his life. They had been married for nine years; four other children had been born but only two, the first son and a daughter had lived beyond childhood. Margaret had cheered his spirits during his long struggle and disappointment. 'I beg that you will not make yourself uneasy,' she had written in answer to a desponding letter, 'though things should not succeed to your wish. If it (the engine) will not do, something else will; never despair.'

In return for her love and care, Watt had been an affectionate husband; indeed, his present work, for which he had not much taste, had been undertaken the better to provide for her and the children. He felt the loss of his wife deeply; after any absence from home he had to nerve himself to enter the house where he would see her no more. In the eighteenth and nineteenth centuries, the loss of a young mother and her child in childbirth was not, as it is now, a rare occurrence. Much suffering was caused through lack of medical knowledge and the bearing of children was haunted by dread.

Watt endeavoured to still his grief by hard work. Some years previously he had visited Birmingham, then as now, a great centre of metal-working. He had been shown over a newly erected works, the 'Soho Manufactury', belonging to Matthew Boulton. Matthew Boulton, who was born in 1728, inherited his father's business as a manufacturer of silver articles, buckles, watch-chains, buttons and 'other trifles'. Boulton enlarged the scope of the work and improved its quality by introducing new and more tasteful designs and by insisting on the best workmanship. The father died when Matthew was 31 years of age, leaving a considerable amount of property as well as the metal-works.

Matthew was fortunate in persuading Anne Robinson, an agreeable young lady with a handsome dowry to marry him. Anne was somewhat above Matthew in social status and her family tried to prevent the marriage but the two had fallen in love. They were very happy together. Matthew was able and good-looking and took a lively interest in art and science. Their home was the meeting-place for a wide circle of men and woman who had an interest in the things of the mind. They formed what was called 'The Lunar Society' because they met in each other's home at that time of the month when the moon was full, a convenience for travelling in a period when streets and roads were unlighted. Many distinguished and famous persons were members: Erasmus Darwin, who was as knowledgable as his famous grandson, Charles Darwin, Josiah Wedgwood, the potter, Joseph Priestley, a pioneer chemist, are only a few examples. The Lunar Society met for discussion. Papers were read on scientific, political, artistic and literary subjects.

Matthew Boulton used the large amount of money at his disposal to found a 'manufactory' at Soho that was the best of its kind. Large quantities of a variety of metal goods were produced, especially those of an ornamental character, such as gold and silver vases and bronze figures. Boulton constantly searched for artistic and tasteful designs; he would attend sales and buy antiques to copy; he spent much time in the British Museum, making drawings of Greek and Roman statues and urns. His work was bought by members of the aristocracy and the royal family. A vase representing Hercules was ordered; Boulton gave instructions that particular attention should be given to it. 'Let it be well gilt, for 'tis the Queen's.'

The Soho works impressed Watt by its size and the good arrangements for efficiency and transport. He envied the excellence of the tools and the skill of the workmen. In Glasgow, the artisans he employed were, he said, 'villianous bad'. On a subsequent visit Watt and Boulton met and the suggestion was made that Boulton should promote the making and selling of Watt's engine. Many other meetings took place and much correspondence passed between the two. They had taken a mutual liking to each other and Boulton gave Watt a few orders. A curious example is, 'One dozen German flutes at 5s. each and a copper digester, £1 10s.'

Boulton was interested in Watt's engine but he had a large and growing business which he had difficulty in financing. Also perhaps, he was not anxious to undertake the launching of a new invention until it had been proved efficient. Eventually, however, an arrangement was come to between the manufacturer and the inventor and during the year following the death of Mrs. Watt a trial engine was in process of erection at the Soho works.

Watt had completed the job on which he was engaged, the survey of the Caledonian Canal. He was, in his own words, 'heartsick of Scotland'. Uncertain of his future, he went to Birmingham to see

how the trial engine was faring. The superior workmanship at Soho and a cast-iron cylinder made by
John Wilkinson, son of the Isaac Wilkinson previously mentioned and now a famous iron-master,
resulted in an engine which promised well. Watt
wrote to his father, 'The business I am about here has
turned out rather successful; the engine I invented is
now going and answers much better than any other
that has been made and I expect the invention will be
very beneficial to me.' Watt was never over-enthusi-
astic and, for him, this modest statement is optimistic.

An agreement was now made with Matthew
Boulton. Boulton undertook to use the resources of
the Soho manufactury to sell the Watt Steam
Engine and to keep the accounts connected with it.
Watt was to superintend the erection of the engine
on the premises of the buyers. He was to receive a
salary of £330 a year. The engine was not sold as such;
its various parts were made to order, some at the Soho
works, some by John Wilkinson or other iron manufacturers. Boulton and Watt sold the right to use the
engine and undertook to maintain it. Further payments were to be received yearly in proportion to
the amount of coal saved by the use of the engine
in comparison with the fuel consumed by the Newcomen. Profits were to be shared on the basis of
one-third to Watt, two-thirds to Boulton. Boulton
also paid some debts owed by Watt in connection
with previous trial engines. It was a clumsy arrangement and caused a lot of future trouble.

Watt now moved to Birmingham with his two children. Boulton had taken a house for them, Regent's Place, not far from the Soho works. It was a large house, three-storied and stood in a garden together with a coach-house and stable. A print shows the smoking chimneys of the works in the background. To this place Watt brought his second wife, Anne. She had been Anne Macgregor and her father was a dyer and bleacher in Glasgow. He had been reluctant to consent to the marriage until the agreement with Boulton had been signed. However, apart from the success of the marriage and the fortune subsequently made by Watt, Macgregor had good cause to rejoice that he had given his consent.

The old method of bleaching by drenching the cloth with sour milk and exposing it to the air for several weeks had been superseded in France by using chlorine as a bleaching agent. Macgregor had heard something of this and, when Watt had occasion to go to France, Macgregor asked him to try and discover particulars. This Watt did; he also helped his future father-in-law in experimenting, with the result that Macgregor had the advantage of being the first bleacher in Britain to use the new and much more economical process.

The second Mrs. Watt was an educated, capable and intelligent woman. She was a good wife though over-careful about the house. It was said that she even taught her two pug dogs to wipe their feet before they went over the threshold. Like many women whose husbands have mechanical tastes, she was exasperated by oil and dirt brought into the house from the workshop. Her husband did not quarrel with her niceties; he took refuge in a garret which he fitted with a bench and tools. It must have troubled him more seriously that, as his son grew older, he and his stepmother could not agree. There were two children by the second marriage, a boy and a girl. Both died of tuberculosis of the lungs before they were fully grown.

In the first year of the Boulton and Watt partnership, orders for three engines were received, one for John Wilkinson's blast-furnaces, one for pumping water from a mine in Staffordshire and one for a distillery in London. The first two worked satisfactorily; the distillery engine gave trouble and Watt had to go himself to put it right. The old trouble of not sufficiently skilled workmen harassed Watt continually. England, it seems, was as bad as Scotland.

The truth is that Watt expected too much. Before machine tools were invented it was exceedingly difficult to get the precision necessary to prevent the escape of steam under pressure. The number of workmen able to do this was very small and the shortage became acute as the demand for the engine increased. After the success of the London engine, orders poured in from Cornwall, where the tin-mines were 'drowning' beyond the power of the Newcomen engine to prevent. Within four years, forty Watt engines had been supplied to Cornwall. They were even more effective than had been expected for, with their use, the mines could go deeper. The tin industry, which had been threatened with ruin, took a new lease of life. The 'giant, steam' had proved its power.

Far from bringing ease and happiness to Watt, this technical success was a source of endless worry, work and financial difficulty. It was almost impossible to get the annual payments from the mine-owners. They, having paid for the engines either discontinued the yearly payments or disputed the amount. It was necessary for Watt to make constant visits to Cornwall to recover debts as well as to erect and maintain the engines sold. Cornwall, at this time, was a remote and isolated part of the kingdom, with few roads, most of them bad. The people were nearer in race to the Welsh than to the English and it was not long since they had spoken a separate language. They had many local laws and customs and a strong sense of neighbourliness among themselves. They were not fond of strangers and seldom co-operated with them. Cornwall was not a rich county apart from the tin-mines and the tin industry had been passing through a difficult time owing to flooding in the mines. Several thousand tin-workers were out of work and the fear of more mines closing lay like a shadow on the districts.

In good times tin-workers earned fair wages but most of their money went in food and, according to

Watt, drinking to excess. In hard times they had few reserves and little chance, locally, of other employment. Whole villages depended on the tin industry. When the mine closed, all suffered. Their houses were small and crowded without sanitation or comfort. In such circumstances, bouts of drinking are not surprising. Watt did not like and could not get on with Cornishmen. For years he spent long periods of time in the county and his letters are full of complaints. The Cornish were, he wrote, mean, jealous and treacherous. 'They have the most ungracious manners of any people I have yet been among.' Every word Watt said was bandied about the village and gossiped over. People talked of him behind his back and spread false rumours.

Watt was intolerant of the way in which the mines were run, not seeing or allowing for the primitive conditions of a long-established industry. Of a mine called 'Cakes and Ale' he wrote: 'The engine (Newcomen) is clumsy and nasty, the houses cracked and everything dripping with water.' Of another mine called 'Wheal Virgin' he wrote that the owners and managers were coarse and unmannered, 'the bulk of them would not be disgraced by being classed with colliers.' Mrs. Watt shared her husband's dislike:

> The spot we are at is the most disagreeable in the whole country. The face of the earth is broken up in ten thousand heaps of rubbish and there is scarce a tree to be seen. . . . In some places my poor husband has been obliged to mount me behind him to go to some of the

places we have been at. I assure you I was not a little perplexed to be set on a great tall horse with a high pillion (cushion).

No suitable house could be found in which they could lodge and the Watts were forced to accept the hospitality of the mine superintendent. Nevertheless, Mrs. Watt was charmed with the Cornish coast, one of the most beautiful in England, and she described a picnic to one of the little bays where only 'twopence apiece was charged for our dinner. You may guess what our fare was like from the cost of it but I never ate a dinner with more relish in my life.'

The Cornishmen were struck with astonishment at the power of the steam-engine. 'All the world are agape', wrote Watt to Boulton, 'to see what it can do.' A large crowd gathered at the Chacewater mine to see the engine commence to work. 'The velocity, violence, magnitude and horrible noise gave universal satisfaction to all beholders, believers nor not.' Watt added that some of the crowd would not have been displeased if the engine had failed. In course of time, some of the hostility died away. The water was being 'forked out' of the mines as never before.

Watt, in spite of his constant grumbles, learned to handle Cornishmen and, what he disliked even more, found methods of negotiating with the mine-owners about payments. These were never very satisfactory though Boulton, who was more accustomed to bargaining and did not dislike it, went to Cornwall to aid Watt. Boulton, more a 'man of the world' than Watt, went round the mines and had many 'friendly conferences' with the managers. He was able to raise a loan on the security of the engines installed. Had the agreements been honoured and regular payments made, both Boulton and Watt would have been spared years of anxiety.

The difficulty of maintaining the steam-engine in working order where there were no suitable craftsmen locally, was met by sending William Murdock from Soho to Cornwall. William Murdock, who afterwards became famous, was the most outstanding of Boulton and Watt's skilled mechanics. His father was a millwright, a highly skilled trade and his son followed his father's calling. When he was 23 years of age Murdock, wishing to gain experience, left his father's shop in Scotland, walked to Birmingham and applied for a job at Soho. He had heard of the new steam-engine.

Boulton, who interviewed him, was impressed by the intelligence of the tall, good-looking young man. Murdock, who was nervous at meeting the important and wealthy Boulton, twiddled his hat round and round in his hands. It was a curious hat, made of wood and Murdock had made and painted it himself. It was evident that he was clever with his hands and inventive and ingenious by nature. Boulton congratulated Murdock on his hat and told him to call again. After a trial, he was engaged. Beginning as a mechanic, he was given more and more responsible work. He became what nowadays would be called technical works manager.

In Cornwall, Murdock was invaluable. Apparently he lived only for the engines. They pursued him in his dreams for he was once found, heaving away at his bedpost, shouting in his sleep, 'Now she goes, lads, now she goes.' He was soon on good terms with the Cornishmen. At first, they tried to bully him but, by offering to 'fight it out' and soundly beating those who accepted the offer, he won their respect. By kindly 'man to man' behaviour he won their affection also. They preferred him to Watt and, illogically, Watt was annoyed at this, though he did not himself care a rap for Cornishmen.

Murdock's wages were £2 a week, a high wage for a working man but not as much as Murdock thought he was worth. He asked for a rise of 2s., not a large sum it would seem. Boulton did not see his way to agreeing; however, he made Murdock a present of ten guineas and obtained another ten for him from the mine-owners, who had a very high opinion of Murdock's character and abilities. Murdock remained loyal to Boulton and Watt though he received offers of better-paid work. As the steam-engine business became financially sound, Murdock's wages were increased. He was not ambitious; money and power meant less to him than the opportunity to use his mechanical and inventive genius but, in his later years, he won a modest prosperity. His small but pleasant house, Sycamore Hill, Handsworth, stood in a garden surrounded by trees. On the lawn stood 'the first piece of iron-toothed gearing ever cast', a curious but appropriate ornament for so devoted a mechanic.

Murdock made many inventions, some successful, some not. He introduced lighting by gas. 'Do you mean to tell us', he was asked, 'that it will be possible to have a light without a wick?' 'Yes, I do indeed,' Murdock firmly answered. During his stay in Cornwall he had conducted many experiments with a view to using inflammable gas obtained from coal for lighting. He had been successful in lighting the house in which he lived and, on returning to Soho, he was authorized by Boulton to install gas lighting in the offices and buildings. During the war with France, the temporary peace of 1802 was celebrated with national rejoicing. The front of the Soho works was brilliantly illuminated by gas, 'to the astonishment and admiration of the public'. Murdock's attempts to use the steam-engine as a means of locomotion, that is, to put it on wheels and so create a 'horse-less carriage', were not successful. Here, he was before his time. Rails were needed to prevent the engine and carriage from being shaken to pieces.

Murdock's ingenious mind and clever hands were constantly at work in improving the mechanical arrangements at Soho, in aiding Watt in his inventions and in a multitude of ploys which his busy and far-ranging interests suggested. On a visit to Manchester, one of the first towns to illuminate the streets with gas, Murdock was invited to dine at the house of a Mr. Fairburn. His host lived some distance from the lighted area of the town. It was a moonless night and the roads were foul. The way passed the newly erected gasworks; Murdock went in, took a pig's bladder from his pocket, filled it with gas, placed the stem of an old tobacco-pipe in the neck of the bladder and so produced a stream of light which enabled Mr. Fairburn and himself to pick their way through the dark and dirty lane.

Many such stories were told about him. Happy in his work and simple in his tastes, unconcerned with problems of profit or finance, Watt often envied Murdock's ease of mind and robust constitution. He outlived Boulton and Watt and served the sons of both as they took over the business. He died in 1839 in his eighty-fifth year. A monument in Handsworth Church commemorates his life and works.

By 1780, the Cornish tin-mines were well supplied with Watt's pumping-engine and this part of the Soho business was beginning to show a fair profit. The Soho works, unfortunately, were doing badly and immense debts had accumulated. Worried, pessimistic, melancholy, nervous and suffering from his usual indigestion, coughs and headaches, Watt was a burden to himself. 'I am quite eat up with the mulligrubs', he wrote to Boulton. His wife was in despair. She, too, wrote to Boulton: 'Whether the badness of his health is owning to the lowness of his spirits or the lowness of his spirits to his bad health, I cannot pretend to tell.' Nevertheless, during this period, an unusually depressed one, even for Watt, his inventive mind continued to be active. He produced work which he regarded as his best.

The steam-engine had been specially adapted for pumping. By a new device Watt succeeded in applying the power produced by the engine to a number of other purposes, tilting blacksmiths' hammers, rolling metals, grinding corn and driving textile machines. Within the next few years orders for the new rotary steam engine were received at an increasing rate. The effect of steam-power on the location of textile-mills has previously been noted. Many other industries, hitherto tied to rivers by the need for water-power, were established in places more convenient for labour, coal and transport. Factories and workshops were concentrated in towns which grew rapidly on or near the coal-fields. By 1800, nearly 300 rotary engines were in use. Industry, it was said, was 'steam mad'. The industrial town, as distinct from the older market town became part of the British pattern of settlement. The industrial 'townscape' was taking shape—a forest of high chimneys above a huddle of mean streets, now a serious problem for the town planner.

Unlike the original steam-engine, the rotary-engine was made at Soho and sold to the customer for an inclusive price, thus avoiding the difficulties connected with extracting annual payments from reluctant users. With the success of the rotary-engine the financial situation at Soho improved. The position was curious. Boulton, who in the course of his many

6(a). *An engine house (see p. 123)*

(b). *The iron founder (see p. 142)*

four Wheel Drill Plow with a Seed and a Manure Hopper was first Invented in the Ye
is now in Use with W.ᵐ Ellis at Little Gaddesden near Hempstead in Hertfordshire where a
View the same. It is so light that a Man may Draw it but Generally drawn by a pony or little

7(a).   *Mr. Coker's hoe (see p. 182)*

  (b).   *The drill plow (see p. 182)*

business undertakings had spent and lost a fortune, was now worse off than his partner. Watt, who had started with no money at all, had saved his profits and refused to be drawn into Boulton's many schemes. With age and prosperity, Watt's health improved; he took a house away from the Soho works and spent the last years of his life happily inventing 'trifles', reading novels and travelling for pleasure. He lived to be 83 years old. He was buried in Handsworth Church, where a monument inscribed with his attainments was erected.

Boulton, to quote his own words, 'must either rub or rust'. Almost until the end of his life, though constantly in pain from stone in the kidney, he tottered down to Soho where his life's interests had been centred. His naturally sunny and optimistic disposition was clouded by pain during his last years and when death came, in 1809, at the age of 81, he was glad to go. The partnership of these two men, Boulton and Watt, so different in upbringing and temperament was cemented by a friendship which survived many trials and some disagreements. It has been said that modern civilization grew from their achievements.

6

Men of Iron

THE use of the steam-engine in the manufacture of an ever-increasing number and variety of goods made heavy demands on the iron industry. The engines were made of iron and the machines driven by the engines came also to be made of metal. The transition from wood to iron for making textile machinery began with the use of water-power. The quickened movement caused the machines to shudder and thump and it was found necessary to strengthen the parts that took the strain. Moreover, wood wore away quickly and, as the joints loosened, the machine was thrown out of true and did not work well.

A contemporary account describing a small factory of about 1800, shows how frustrating the defects of these early machines could be and also shows a mechanic at work. Such accounts are very rare. The writer, William Radcliffe, had a number of textile machines which constantly got out of order and which he was trying to improve. He employed a mechanic, Thomas Johnson of Bredbury, the son of a hand-loom weaver. Bredbury is on one of the roads which cross the Pennines. At the time of which Radcliffe was writing, coal had been mined in Bredbury for over a century and a new and deeper mine had just been opened. Pack-horse trains passed along the road and also wagons, for the road was a turnpike and had a hard surface.

Pack- and wagon-horses provided plenty of work for the smith and there were several forges in the village. The local coal was used in shoeing horses and for making pans, kettles, pokers and the usual ware turned out at that time by village blacksmiths. It is possible that young Johnson had been apprenticed to a local smith but more likely that he had picked up some knowledge of iron-working by hanging about the forges. He was, according to Radcliffe, a young man of unsatisfactory character and a trial to his father, the hand-loom weaver. He could not settle down to regular work and he drank heavily; he would go off for several days on a drinking bout. Nevertheless, he was clever mechanically; 'My Conjuror', Radcliffe called him. He could 'fettle' (mend) a machine and he could improve on Radcliffe's instruction and make suggestions about the building of machines. Johnson and Radcliffe between them worked out several new devices for extending the usefulness of the power-loom and a patent was taken out in Johnson's name.

When Johnson was missing from the factory, Radcliffe searched for him in the various public houses that Johnson frequented and, or so it was said, would throw a bucket of water over him to 'sober him up'. Radcliffe was anxious that no details of the improvements they were making to the loom should be known, for he did not want his competitors to take advantage of his ideas. Johnson, however, when 'in drink' would talk, so the room in which the experiments were made was kept locked and sometimes Johnson was locked in with them.

There must have been many mechanics like Johnson, ingenious and contriving and not too hidebound by the conventions of a trade to try new adventures, not of course, necessarily with Johnson's failings. Radcliffe's career well illustrates the hazards of business during the industrial revolution. For some time he did well, extending his factory until he was employing 400 people but later he was ruined and bankrupt. He spent the remaining years of his life in writing long letters to the newspapers praising himself, accusing his successful rivals of stealing his ideas and blaming the government for not protecting the cotton industry.

Several kinds of iron-workers took a hand in making the new machines. Robert Owen, the model employer mentioned previously, first saw a spinning-machine in the workshop of a man called Jones who made large wire frames for ladies' bonnets. Owen who, when young, was a draper's assistant, went to collect a batch of frames. Noticing the strange machines he inquired about them and Jones explained how they worked. Jones told Owen that he had a number on order and that they were in great demand. Owen was interested and Jones, who was short of capital offered Owen a partnership for £100, the two to develop the machine-making side of the business. This was in 1790, when small-scale businesses were usual.

Owen, who was only 19 years old, had not sufficient money himself but he borrowed £100 from his brother. The new firm, Owen and Jones, rented a workshop, bought the materials—iron, brass and wood—on credit and were soon employing forty metal-workers. Hundreds of such small ventures were made about this time. They increased the demand for metal.

Throughout the eighteenth century Britain was intermittently at war with Spain or France for the possession of colonies. In general, Britain was the victor. In 1776, the American colonists declared their independence and a war, unsuccessful for Britain, was fought in an endeavour to keep them under British rule. From 1792–1815 Britain was almost continually engaged in a large-scale war with France from which Britain emerged victorious. Quantities of guns of various kinds, including cannon, were needed during these wars but, in the intervals of peace, the demand slackened. Thus, the metal industries were alternately stimulated and depressed. Boom conditions were followed by loss of orders and unemployment.

During the wars, the price of iron rose; iron-workers were in demand. The Birmingham district, where guns had been made for centuries, reached a 'top pinnacle of prosperity'. Iron was sold as fast as it could be made 'at profit enough'; trains of wagons waited for the furnaces to be tapped and the iron was carried to the gun-makers while it was still hot. In South Wales, Cumberland and Scotland new furnaces were erected. In the iron-fields of Staffordshire, Yorkshire and Northumberland the weight of metal produced and the number of people employed increased with spectacular rapidity.

During the intervals of peace large fortunes were whittled away or wiped out by large losses. The savings from high wages disappeared in long spells of short time or unemployment. Before the outbreak of war with the American colonists, trade was particularly bad. A large quantity of ironware was sent to America in normal times; now, the colonists were refusing to buy British goods. One British merchant, who usually sent £50,000 worth of nails in a year, reported that orders from America were not coming in and he had 300 workmen unemployed. 'The trade of Birmingham is so dead', wrote Matthew Boulton, 'that the London wagons have to make up their loading with coals for want of (ironware) merchandise.' Boulton, himself, was seriously embarrassed financially and even so large and famous a works as the Carron Company were near to bankruptcy.

Distress in the iron districts was reflected in other areas. Writing in 1775, John Wesley, who was travelling about the country on a preaching mission, recorded in his *Journal* that he had seen, 'East, West, North and South' thousands of people 'creeping up and down like walking shadows.' Some had perished for want of bread. The Darbys of Coalbrookdale were, you will remember, Quakers, members of the Society of Friends who oppose war on religious grounds. The Darbys made no cannon or fire-arms. At the time of the American War of Independence the head of the firm was the third Abraham Darby, the grandson of the Abraham who had coked coal for smelting iron.

The works at Coalbrookdale had grown and prospered. The third Abraham, rather than make munitions, turned to bridge building. He built the first bridge to be made of cast iron. It spanned the River Severn. All the iron with which it was made was cast at Coalbrookdale. The bridge took three years to build, provided work other than munitions for the employees and a quicker and easier means of communication between Staffordshire and Shropshire. A new town, Ironbridge, soon sprang up close by.

Several iron bridges were built by other firms during the eight years' peace between the American war and the long war with France; these and other new uses for iron, such as water-pipes and rails for wagons in works and mines, helped the industry through the slump. The new steam-engines were also a factor, though not an important one till nearly the end of the century. By that time the country was engaged in a war in which heavy guns and munitions of all kinds were used as never before. The iron industry reached a new peak of expansion. Production from the furnaces doubled in the ten years between 1796–1806. The slump that followed the Battle of Waterloo was correspondingly disastrous. On a larger scale than before, works closed down or went on short time; iron-masters lost heavily and workmen and their families used up the savings of years, sold their furniture and wandered starving about the district. This slump lasted nearly ten years.

Nevertheless, in spite of setbacks and periods of near ruin, there was an immense overall expansion in the iron industry during the industrial revolution. In the middle years of the eighteenth century the output of bar iron from the forges was estimated at 18,000 tons a year. Fifty years later, furnaces were turning out 250,400 tons of pig-iron. These figures show not only the increase in production; they indicate a change in the way the metal was extracted and worked. New methods and processes had made the increase possible. These changes affected the way in which the industry was organized and the lives of those engaged in it. Most, though not all, of the tonage shown for the earlier period was produced in small furnaces and was subsequently worked by individual blacksmiths at their own forges. Most of the tonnage of the later period was the result of immensely larger undertakings.

Until the eighteenth century, the method of smelting iron from ironstone and making it into wrought or cast iron or steel had hardly altered for hundreds of years. Beginning with Abraham Darby's use of coke instead of charcoal for smelting, many inventions and improvements gradually followed. Changes in the iron industry were not as rapid as those in textiles but, by the end of the eighteenth century, fiercer furnaces, the crucible process for steel, the use of power for puddling and rolling and other inventions had enormously increased efficiency. Larger masses of metal could be handled with less labour and in a shorter time. The inventive genius of many men and much patient effort over the years were devoted to achieve these successes. Outstanding names are Benjamin Huntsman, Henry Cort, John Wilkinson.

Benjamin Huntsman was born in 1704. As a young man he was a clockmaker in Doncaster, Yorkshire. He also engaged in the simple surgery of the day and was an occulist. For several years he experimented in making the differing kinds of steel, trying to make one that would be better for the springs of clocks and take a keener cutting edge for the knives he used in operations, especially those on the eye. About 1740, he moved to Sheffield where he succeeded in making a steel of superior quality by keeping the fluid iron at an intense heat for many hours. This was done in small pots of clay, less than a foot in height, called crucibles. Huntsman mixed several kinds of clay together to enable the crucibles to withstand the heat. He also invented a flux, a mixture of materials that assist the particles of metal to fuse. Steel produced by

Huntsman's process was better than any yet produced for springs, razors, penknives and tools.

Huntsman tried to keep his process secret but his steel was so superior that other manufacturers tried to find out how it was made. The story goes that Samuel Walker, one of three brothers who had an ironworks in Sheffield, disguised himself as a tramp and begged to be allowed to warm himself at Huntsman's furnace. The furnace man, in pity, gave him leave and Walker, watching with sharp eyes, saw the details of the process. Very soon after this is said to have happened, the Walkers were making steel by Huntsman's method and others followed. Nevertheless, Huntsman and his son established a firm which has survived until today and which still has a reputation for making steel of the highest quality for its special purpose.

Huntsman was a shy retiring man not anxious to move in circles where he was not at ease. He was not interested in 'cutting a figure' in society and even when the Royal Society offered him a Fellowship he did not accept it. When he was 70 years of age the works were removed to larger premises at Attercliffe, a suburb of Sheffield. Huntsman died seven years afterwards in 1776. His son and his son's son succeeded him.

Pig iron gets its homely name from the form that the molten metal was made to take as it ran from the furnace. At the mouth of the furnace there was a central channel of sand with side channels at right angles to it. The central channel was the sow and the side channels were the little pigs sucking at the old sow's side. The liquid iron flowed along the channels and, when cool enough, was broken into 'pigs'. A great deal of hand labour was necessary to convert the pigs into a tough resistant wrought iron that could be used for such things as nails, horseshoes, rails, boilers, gears and crankshafts, all goods which get a great deal of knocking about. Henry Cort invented two processes that simplified, quickened and cheapened the conversion of pig into wrought iron.

Instead of much hammering and reheating, pigs were laid on the floor in the furnace, heated by a fierce blast which struck down from the roof and worked into clotted lumps, 'as the stirring of cream' makes it into butter. This process is called puddling. The lumps were passed through grooved rollers to squeeze out impurities, so producing in a single operation a long bar of malleable iron.

Henry Cort patented the processes but other men had been working on the same lines and his claim to be the original inventor was challenged. He was an unfortunate man. Born in 1740 in Lancaster, at the age of 25 he went to London. He was engaged as an agent for buying guns for the Navy. The best metal for guns was imported from Europe so Cort began experimenting in order to improve the quality of English metal. For ten years he laboured on the problem and, in 1775, he erected a forge near Farnham, Hampshire, where he was better able to try out his ideas. He used water-power for some of the processes. In 1782 he went to Soho to consult Boulton about the possibility of a steam-engine to help out his water-supply.

Boulton wrote to Watt, 'We had a visit today from a Mr. Cort who says he has found some grand secret in the making of iron, by which he can double the quantity at the same expense and in the same time as usual.' Cort had told Boulton that he did most of the 'smith work' for the King's naval yard. He was, thought Boulton, 'a simple good-natured man but not very knowing'.

These qualities are not the best for dealing with unscrupulous men. When it was discovered that Cort's partner, Samuel Jellicoe, had used thousands of pounds of public money to invest in the business, Cort was ruined. Jellicoe was paymaster for the Navy. Cort had made over the patent rights to him in return for the capital investment and the patent was confiscated by the Treasurer of the Navy. Cort had known nothing about his partner's dishonesty so, after many appeals, the government granted him a pension of £200 a year. On this not very generous grant, Cort had to keep a wife and a very large family. He died in 1800 and the pension ceased to be paid. His wife was destitute. Large fortunes were being made in the iron industry as the result of Cort's discoveries but an appeal to the iron-masters for help for his widow and children only brought in £871 10s.

The title of this chapter aptly describes the character of John Wilkinson; it has been said that he was made of cast iron. He was the son of the Isaac Wilkinson who was described in a previous chapter as carrying molten iron to his foundry in the Lake District. John Wilkinson was born in 1728 and as soon as he was old enough he began to help his father and learn the trade. When John was about 12 years of age his father erected a furnace; he could now both smelt and cast iron for his growing business in iron-ware. John and his brother helped their father. They were an energetic and ingenious family; they cut a small canal for bringing fuel to the works and made an iron boat, a very early use of metal for this purpose.

About the middle of the eighteenth century, the Wilkinsons moved south to Bersham, near St. Asaph, North Wales. They leased a furnace and made 'guns, cannon, fire-engines, pipes' and rollers for crushing sugar. In 1770, Isaac Wilkinson, having either died or retired, the brothers enlarged their operations by erecting furnaces in many different districts, Cumberland, Cornwall, the 'Black Country' and also in France and Germany. They leased coal- and iron-mines and worked them to supply their furnaces with the raw material. As iron-masters they were among the richest and most powerful in the country.

John Wilkinson made a great variety of iron commodities, many of them requiring great quantities o iron for their construction, so far had he travelled from the pots and pans of his childhood. He is most famous for the making of the large cannon which were being increasingly used in war. In 1774, he invented a new method of boring. This made possible a greater accuracy of aim. Wilkinson's cannon were supplied to the British government, the East India Company, and many of the countries of Europe, including, so it was said, France, even when Britain and France were at war. 'The cannon's opening roar' at Waterloo brought terror and devastation on both sides of the battle line.

The superior accuracy of boring at Wilkinson's forges was one of the factors in bringing Watt's steam-engine to success. Shortly after Wilkinson opened his Bilston works, Boulton ordered some cylinders from him. We have seen how frustrated Watt had been by badly fitting work on the engine. From Wilkinson's cylinders there was no escape of steam. Watt was delighted and Boulton wrote to the firm who had previously supplied them, 'Wilkinson hath bored us several cylinders almost without error'; they did not vary 'the thickness of an old shilling in no part'. A warning was given that no further orders could be expected.

Wilkinson was a sharp man of business. His prices were higher than those of other iron-masters, he demanded prompt payment and he gave no discount. He was a hard and ruthless man as unyielding as the ironware he made so excellently. Few people had a good word to say about his character and there were many scandals about his private life. He had several illegitimate children. His immense wealth enabled him to provide handsomely for them. One of them, a daughter, was married to a Legh, of Lyme, Cheshire. She became the mother of the first Lord Newton.

Boulton, who could get on with almost everybody, gave Wilkinson guarded and faint praise. 'I can't say', he wrote to Watt, 'but that I admire John Wilkinson for his decisive, clear and distinct character, which is, I think, a first-rate one of its kind.' Boulton and Wilkinson did a considerable amount of business together over thirty years to their mutual benefit. The first Watt engine to be used for another purpose than pumping was made for Wilkinson for his blast furnace. It was a striking success and Wilkinson bought others and recommended them to his business acquaintances not, perhaps, without regard to his own interest. Boulton and Watt advised their customers to have the engine parts made at his works. Wilkinson seldom dealt with people without thinking of some return to himself.

The inventions and enterprise of Huntsman, Cort, Wilkinson and many others expanded production and cheapened iron. An increasing number of workpeople were dependent on the industry. It is not possible to give details of their personal lives but some idea of the conditions of their work and the way in which they lived can be gained from accounts made at the time. In 1842, rather later than the period dealt with in this book, an inquiry was made into the condition of children employed in ironworks. With caution, the report issued by the commission of inquiry can be used to give information about the earlier period.

Dozens of different types of workers were employed in the iron industry, blast-furnacemen, forgemen, puddlers, rollers, moulders, smiths, enginemen, labourers and the men who worked in supplying the raw material, ironstone- and coal-miners, limestone quarriers, carters. Women were employed but not in great numbers; they were generally the wives of labourers. Boys, too, learning a trade or doing odd jobs were employed from the age of 9; the work was too strenuous for very young children to be of much use and the amount of child-labour was small compared with that in other industries.

All accounts of the iron-workers agree on their outstanding strength. They were described as being 'men of athletic make and great bodily vigour' and, though the work was exceedingly heavy, it was not unhealthy. It was compared favourably, in this respect, with work in the textile factories which 'tended to produce a feeble and degenerate race of men'. But, in handling masses of molten metal, accidents were bound to happen with terrible consequences. A furnaceman might 'take the iron' that is, the boiling fluid spattered over him with great force, penetrating and burning holes in the flesh. This might make him permanently unable to work or cause his death. No inquests were held on accidents.

The coroner would be informed and, if there were

8. *A cellar dwelling, interior and exterior*

9. *A street scene*

no suggestion of foul play, a certificate would be issued without further inquiry. 'Taking the iron' was generally the result of the bursting of a worn-out furnace door. The workmen complained that, to keep down costs, furnace doors were not replaced sufficiently often. The attitude of taking accidents as a matter of course, a hazard of the industry, applied also in mining.

In districts where the industry was well established, relationships between master and workmen were, on the whole, good. The Darbys of Coalbrookdale and the Crowleys of Newcastle regarded their workmen and their families with a paternal eye. They provided a doctor, a school and insurance against sickness and old age towards which a small sum was deducted from the workmen's wages. Efforts were made to keep the men employed during slack periods. At Coalbrookdale, wagons running on wooden rails were used for transport. During a spell of bad trade, iron rails were made and substituted; the wooden ones were kept so that, if there were a sudden demand for iron, they could be laid down again and the iron refashioned for sale.

Wages were good and compared well with other industries. They varied from over £2 a week for highly skilled and responsible work to 8s. or 9s. for labourers. There was the added advantage of a low-rented house. As far as coal was concerned, it was said that the men often 'helped themselves to it' but, even when they paid for it, the price was low. The 'truck' system was usual; that is, wages were partly paid in tickets or tokens which could only be spent at a shop owned by the employer. This might not be a disadvantage if, as sometimes happened, prices were kept low but an unscrupulous employer could charge high because the shopper had no alternative. The truck system encouraged debt and increased the power of the employer over his workmen.

The iron-master's power was indeed great. Jobs, houses, credit, were theirs to give or withhold; they controlled the price of provisions; they were land-owners and magistrates. All, even the best employers among them, fiercely resisted any attempt to limit their power. Very few attempts at forming unions were made by the ironworkers of the eighteenth century. A tradition still lingered of the craft guild of former times. Skilled workers were paid piecework rates or a bonus on production. They frequently employed and paid their assistants who were often their sons. Thus, they tended to regard themselves not as employees but as independent workers long after the reality of independence was gone. Moreover, trade unions had been strongly opposed by the masters when they appeared in trades connected with the iron industry—nail- and scissors-making or mining.

It may well be, however, that the ironworkers made attempts to strengthen their position in bargaining with the iron-masters by forming trade unions and that the records have been lost. The earliest record to survive points to this. The 'Friendly Society of Iron Founders' was formed on 6 February 1809 at Bolton, Lancashire. From the first the members engaged in trade union activity and, to ensure secrecy, the books of the Society were buried in the peat of the neighbouring moors. At this time trade unions were illegal and friendly societies were often used as a cloak. The struggle of the working class to organize will be described in a later chapter.

The working hours in the iron industry were very long, at Coalbrookdale from 6 a.m. to 6 p.m. with breaks amounting to $1\frac{1}{2}$ hours in the course of the day. At Crowley's works the men began work at 5 a.m. and finished at 8 p.m., a $13\frac{1}{2}$-hour day, allowing for breaks. If, as was usual, the furnaces were kept going day and night, night work would be worked alternate weeks. The night-shift would work 24 hours on Sunday at a stretch so that they did not overlap with the new day-shift. Some iron-masters allowed the furnace to go out for a few hours on Sundays, thus giving the workmen a rest but this cost money and the 7-day week was more usual.

There does not seem to have been a regular working day for boys. They worked as required or until their fathers thought they had done as much as they should. An iron-master, William Matthews, who employed about fifty boys at Kingswinford, Staffordshire, said of them, 'They work their own time; if they are tired they go home and their fathers do their business, but generally they work about six or seven hours and sometimes eight or net; they work and

153

play pretty much as they like, subject to the control of their parents.'

Many odd jobs about the ironworks were done by boys, women and, occasionally, by girls—holding horses' heads while the wagons were filled or emptied, picking small pieces of iron from the dross and returning it to the furnace, handing tools to the ironworkers. Women and girls made bags and baskets for the pack-horses and brewed large quantities of ale in the work's brewhouse. Iron-making is thirsty work and most iron-masters supplied ale at cost price to men working at furnace or forge. When the work was particularly hard, a free allowance would be issued.

The good relationship between master and men in the older iron-fields of England was not to be found in South Wales. English ironworks, with some exceptions, had grown through a couple of centuries from small beginnings. Though enormously increased in size, growth had been gradual enough for a sense of community to be preserved. In South Wales, at Merthyr Tydfil, Dowlais and Cyfartha, English iron-masters erected huge furnaces and forges and imported thousands of ironworkers. This change in the Welsh valleys was described in 1831 in the *Monmouthshire Merlin*. 'The district through which our paper circulates is no longer an unknown nook, a pretty hole and corner of the kingdom. It is the centre of important speculations and great trade.'

It was also the home of great masses of people, most

154

of them strangers to one another. The houses had been built without regard for comfort, health or the decencies of life. All around were the furnaces whose smoke clouded the air and whose flames lit the night sky Huge slag-heaps lay in humps on the hillside; as more slag was added they towered above the houses almost at the doors. There were no shops, everything had to be bought at the employers' stores. Some idea of life in such a place can be had from the following description:

> The interior of the houses is, on the whole, clean. Food, clothing, furniture—those wants, the supply of which depends on the exertions of each individual, are tolerably well supplied. It is those comforts which only a governing body can bestow that are here totally absent. The footways are seldom flagged, the streets are ill-paved and with bad materials and are not lighted. The drainage is very imperfect; there are few underground sewers, no house drains and the open gutters are not regularly cleaned out. Dust bins and similar receptacles for filth are unknown; the refuse is thrown into the street.

An open and nearly stagnant gutter 'moved slowly before the doors'. Water had to be carried from springs on the hillsides or taken from the river which was 'charged with filth of the upper houses and works'. There was serious overcrowing; several families lived and slept together, 'sometimes sixteen in one chamber'.

Such conditions were aggravated by hostility between Welsh and English; the Welsh resented the presence of the English and the English despised the Welsh. Heavy drinking was usual and drunken fights often broke out. The Welsh coal- and iron-fields had a bad reputation for law-breaking and disorder, immorality was said to be common and thrift entirely absent, wages being spent as soon as earned and nothing saved for a 'rainy day'.

The 'governing body' mentioned in the quotation from the *Merlin*, who could have provided better social conditions, were the iron-masters. They seem to have thought of little else than making iron and building up a fortune. Richard Crawshay 'started from scratch' and died worth 1½ million. He was a Yorkshire farmer's son and ran away from home to London. He won some money in a lottery and bought a partnership in the Cyfartha ironworks. In 1787 Crawshay was producing 500 tons of bar iron. Twenty years afterwards the output was 10,000 tons.

This colossal expansion is the background to the overcrowding in the workmen's homes, the lack of sanitation and the bad water supply. It would have been difficult for an enlightened authority to keep pace with the demands of the influx of workers implied by these figures. Here, no effort was made. Crawshay's huge 'castle' was only a few miles from the squalid scene described above. As well as the Cyfartha furnaces, he owned an estate of 4,000 acres.

John Guest, who came from Shropshire, was the first Englishman to establish an ironworks in Wales. His son, Josiah John, born in 1785, was first manager and, later, proprietor of Dowlais, one of the largest concerns in the industry. He had the good fortune to marry a lady of culture and learning. She was the daughter of the ninth Earl of Lindsey. Several iron-masters who had made fortunes married into the aristocracy. At the time of her marriage, Lady Charlotte was 21 years old; her husband was more than double her age. Belonging to an ancient noble Scottish family and brought up in Scotland, she found little that was congenial in the industrialized Welsh valleys or in the society of the iron-masters or their wives.

She was gentle and kindly and began to interest herself in the families of the ironworkers and miners. She built a school for the children and visited those who were sick. She supplied comforts and food for those too old to work. In doing this she learnt to speak Welsh and she became interested in the language and history of the Welsh people. Within six years of her marriage, she had published a translation into English of the Mabinogion, a collection of Welsh legends. Lady Charlotte's life was in sharp contrast to her grim surroundings. She collected old china, fans and playing-cards and became an authority on their history and development. She presented many valuable specimens to the British Museum.

This remarkable and attractive lady also took an intelligent interest in her husband's work. Though not an outstanding inventor, Guest made several improvements in the manufacture of iron and steel in the fields of chemistry and engineering. On his death in 1852, Lady Guest took over the management of the Dowlais works. Three years after her husband's death she married Charles Scheiber, a doctor of medicine. She lived to be 83 years old and her memory still lingers in Dowlais.

Two industries, mining and engineering, are closely connected with iron-making. As the output of iron increased, so also mining and engineering expanded. Indeed, mechanical engineering in the modern sense, had its beginning in the need for greater accuracy and precision in the making of engines and power-driven machines. Before the industrial revolution the equivalent of the engineer was the millwright who made and repaired flour-mills. Millwrights and other metal-workers had to train themselves in new skills and, in turn, train apprentices. William Murdock, Watt's 'right hand' at Soho, trained a generation of engineers. A body of engineering knowledge was slowly built up by trial and error.

In the early years of the nineteenth century, under the leadership of a group of brilliant engineers, London became a nursery of skilled engineers with an all-round knowledge of the craft. The workshops were not large by modern standards; few employed more than 100 men and most of the work was still done by hand. In several stages and taking thirty years to develop, machine tools were evolved which cut out a great deal of handwork. A machine tool is a tool operated by a machine of which it is a part; it takes the place of the skilled hand, works much more quickly and with greater accuracy. Unlike the hand, it never tires.

A committee of inquiry into the export of tools and machinery reported in 1825, 'Men and boys in almost any number may be readily instructed in the making of machines' by using machine tools. It was possible to employ 'common labourers, who might rapidly become skilled' on the now simplified processes.

Towards the end of the period dealt with in this book, therefore, the mechanization of engineering was well on its way but a fuller development took place in the second half of the nineteenth century. Only a brief outline of the beginnings of modern engineering can be given here.

The decisive events were, perhaps, the setting up in Manchester of two machine-tool workshops in 1833 and 1834. Whitworth and Nasmyth became famous in the world of mechanical engineering; they were followed by Platts of Oldham and many others. Joseph Whitworth was born in Stockport in 1803. At the age of 14 he went into his uncle's cotton-mill to learn spinning and, such was his ability, when he reached 18 years, he was made manager. He was more interested in the machinery than in manufacturing cotton thread; he left the mill and worked for a while in Manchester, 'on the bench'.

To gain experience he went to London where he worked for Maudsleys, a firm noted for its machine work. At the age of 30 he returned to Manchester. He made and also gave away large sums of money. Whitworth Scholarships were endowed to enable young engineers to be trained; baths and an art gallery were provided from the £500,000 left in his will for the benefit of the people of Manchester and district.

James Nasmyth, the son of a Scottish portrait painter, like Whitworth, went to London to work under Maudsley. At his machine-tool works in Manchester he invented and introduced the steam-hammer, a machine for making nuts for screwheads, a flexible shaft and a number of other improvements to machine tools. A versatile man, he was interested in astronomy and wrote a book on *The Moon*.

South-east Lancashire became a centre of engineering as the result of the development of machine tools. Besides textiles, the district produced all kinds of machines, engines and munitions of war. Workers from Scotland, Wales and from all over England flocked in seeking jobs. The following extracts from the autobiography of Thomas Wood show this happening. He was born in 1822 at Bingley, Yorkshire. His father was a labourer who worked on the roads and about the estate of a local landowner. He earned 10s. a week 'supplemented by gifts from the Hall of blankets, coats and an occasional pot of dripping or a plate of broken meat'.

Thomas had two years at school and learned to read and write. He then joined his sisters in working at a woollen-mill in Bingley. Thomas hated the mill and after six years of endurance he begged his father to find him another job. Thomas was then 14 years old. By a great effort his father found the money for an apprenticeship to a mechanic. 'It caused as much remark among our neighbours as it would now if I put a son to be a doctor', wrote Thomas, thirty years later. The mechanic, David Clayton was, according to Thomas, irritable, poor and wicked. Nevertheless, under him Thomas became a skilled craftsman. When he had 'served his time', he went on tramp seeking work. He was on the road for a month, saw 'hundreds out of work' and was regarded 'as an enthusiast for seeking work when so many were out'. The last day he walked forty miles in pouring rain. Thomas tells a moving story of how his aged aunt washed his feet, dried his clothes, fed him with bread and milk and put him to bed. This was in 1843.

The old mechanics' workshops were suffering from the competition of the new engineering. Clayton, his old master, offered Thomas a job at a low wage but, Thomas wrote, 'I heard about new tools, new machines and new ways of working. So one Friday . . . I walked to Hebden Bridge and took a train for Rochdale, my first railway ride.' The carriages were like cattle-trucks open to the rain and the sparks from the engine. Thomas walked from Rochdale to Oldham and was taken on immediately at Platts, one of the largest machine-shops in England. 'It was with fear', he wrote, 'that I commenced work for a firm who employed near 2,000 hands, whose tools were mostly Whitworth's make—I who had never worked in a shop with more than eight or ten men and with country made tools, the best of which Platts would have thrown away as utterly useless.' Working with a machine tool and doing one kind of work only, Thomas quickly adapted himself to turning out large quantities of specialized work. Thomas Wood was typical of a generation of craftsmen who became mechanical engineers.

Rather curiously, coal-mining, the other industry closely connected with iron-making, remained almost unaltered throughout the industrial revolution. The demand for coal increased enormously. Output rose from about 5 million tons in 1750 to over 10 million in 1800. By 1830 over 50 million tons were being produced and, as the railways spread over Britain, output doubled and doubled again. All these tons of coal were won from the coal-seams by men using a pick and shovel. Squatting on their heels or lying on their backs they hacked the coal loose and shovelled it into wagons. The wagons were 'hurried' along trackways by boys, girls or women who were harnessed to the wagons by leather thongs which passed over their shoulders and between their legs. In some mines the galleries or passages were so low that the 'hurriers' crawled on their hands and knees.

In order to ventilate the mines, trap-doors were placed at intervals along the trackways. These were attended by boys and girls who pulled a string to open or shut the trap as the wagons passed along. Of all the sad, distressing and inhuman demands made on children during the industrial revolution, those made on the little trappers seem to have been the most grim and terrible. Young children of from 5 to 8 years of age sat for twelve hours in total darkness and solitude except for the occasional word and glimpse of light as the wagons came through. Mines could not be safely lighted by any means then available; gases were present which would explode if they came in contact with a naked flame. Some light was, of course, essential and candles were used though sparingly; explosions and loss of life were a common occurrence.

Although there were no revolutionary changes in the miners' work, some improvements were introduced. In 1815, Humphry Davy, a pioneer chemist in the study of gas, invented the miner's safety lamp. The flame was contained within a fine wire gauze. This prevented the gas from exploding. The lamp was strapped to the miner's head or could be placed about the mine. Unfortunately, the use of the safety lamp made it possible to work the deeper and more dangerous mines; its main result was a greater production of coal. Pumping water from mines has previously been described. The early method of hauling coal to the surface by a rope and windlass or carrying it up a series of ladders was gradually discontinued and the steam-engine was used to pump the water to a water-wheel which raised the coal.

Later, the steam-engine was used to lift the coal directly by steam-power.

The miners and their helpers were lowered into the mine and brought back to the surface by the same winding tackle that raised the coal. Sometimes they used the coal-baskets but usually they swung free on the rope with one leg stuck through a loop, one man above another with boys, girls and women astride their knees. Each man clung with one hand to the rope and used the other to prevent collision with the shaft wall. Inevitably, accidents were common; they became more frequent and disastrous as the mines got deeper. In mines where the galleries were high enough, ponies led by children drew sledges or waggons from the coal-face to the bottom of the shaft.

As with the miners' work, so with the miners' lives, there was no great alteration throughout the industrial revolution. The number of people employed in the industry increased but the number employed in any one mine remained small. Few pits were worked by more than fifteen miners until the end of the eighteenth century and the increase in the nineteenth century was slow and gradual. The landscape of a typical coal-field in the eighteenth century would show the winding gear of numbers of small pits clustered about a colliery with, near by, rows of miners' cottages. In the north of England, the cottages were of only one story—one room on either side of the door and a 'lean-to' at the back. As more pits were sunk, more cottages were built and mining villages developed, with shop, public-house, chapel, men, women and children all dependent on coal.

The nature of the miners' work made for a strong sense of community, neighbourly interdependence and comradeship. It also isolated them from people otherwise employed. Even when other industries were near at hand as, for example, in the Potteries or south-east Lancashire the miners remained and were thought to be a race apart. To potters or textile-workers, miners seemed wild, ignorant and dirty.

Miners had a measure of control over the conditions of their work. A gang of miners would contract with the mineowner or lessee to work a pit or get a certain amount of coal and would appoint one of the gang to be their leader. They worked as they chose, generally about seven hours a day until the contract was completed and divided the proceeds among themselves. In the nineteenth century, the leader became a 'butty' who picked his gang and paid them; the independence of the working miner was lost.

In Scotland and in some of the mine-fields of the north of England, the miner had little independence to lose. Until nearly the end of the eighteenth century, many Scottish mineowners had legal rights over the miners and their families that made them little better than serfs. They were bound to work the mines and could be brought back and punished if they ran away. The 'bondage' miners were freed by stages and the last remnants of bondage were abolished in 1799.

In the mines owned by the Duke of Bridgewater, the Earl of Northumberland and other estates in the north, miners worked on a yearly bond. A certain sum was paid at the beginning of the year and the remaining earnings were paid when the year was completed. Miners were almost invariably in debt at the end of the term, for they obtained food, clothing and whatever else they needed on credit at a shop owned by the employer. They were obliged to renew the bond in order to pay what they owed. This might and generally did, go on for a lifetime and the miner would die in debt. The yearly bond for miners was discontinued by slow degrees. In spite of the disadvantages the miners clung to the system because it gave a measure of security. It had disappeared from most mine-fields by the middle of the nineteenth century. It can be said that though the miners did not go through an industrial revolution, they carried one on their bent backs.

7

Farms and Farmworkers

IT is impossible to give a general description of British farming and farm life during the industrial revolution. It differed from district to district, from farm to farm. Many factors, historical and geographical, enter into the story. Only one broad statement can safely be made: the amount of food produced from the land greatly increased. With a population that more than doubled between 1760 and 1830, British farmland continued to supply almost all the food that was eaten. Very little was imported, mainly tea, sugar and other articles that could not be home-grown. During the long wars with France, food was scarce and dear but there was no actual famine.

The soil of England is as varied as its scenery. In the course of a day's journey by car, we can travel over chalk downs, plains of loam or clay, gritstone and limestone hills and river valleys with deep rich silt. The mountains of Wales, Scotland and the Lake District have a shallow covering of soil, not suitable for ploughing but which can pasture sheep and cattle. The fenland of Cambridgeshire and Lincolnshire has a soil so deep and rich that vegetables with long roots flourish in it. Climate also varies; there is more rain and less sunlight in the north than in the south.

Methods of cultivating land vary accordingly and always have done so. Some districts grow crops; some produce beef, mutton and pork; some specialize in dairying or milk. At the present time with one or two exceptions, farming is carried on in individual farms owned or rented by the farmer. This has not always been so. Until the end of the eighteenth century, there was a sharp division in the way in which farming was organized. The open field villages, which were described in Chapter 2, lay mainly in the corn-growing areas. Outside these areas, over the centuries, individual farms had been gradually established on waste land, in clearings in the forests and in districts suitable for cattle-raising or dairying. Even in the corn-growing areas there were many individual farms. The enclosures of the eighteenth century, which completely reorganized the open field village and altered the lives of the villagers, did not affect the individual farms.

The increase in population and the industrial revolution had far-reaching effects on agriculture. There were more mouths to feed; under the domestic system many people raised at least some of their own food; the factory worker could not. Again the picture varies. Farms which were near to the industrial areas could easily sell everything they could produce and

168

if they were near enough could bring their produce
to the market in farm carts and sell it directly to the
customer. Farmers remote from large centres oʃ
population had to depend on merchants or middlemen. Their profit and the cost of transport meant a
lower price for the farmer.

Before the industrial revolution, London was the
greatest and, for some districts, the only market to
which agricultural produce was sent. As the demand
from the industrial areas increased, new lines of communication were opened to 'feed' new markets. A
good example of this comes from the records of an
estate in the south of Cheshire. Cheshire cheese had
been sent to London from as early as the sixteenth
century. Cheese keeps and travels well and even im-
proves with keeping. Cheese for the London market
had become the mainstay of Cheshire farming in the
eighteenth century. It was sold in bulk to a factor
and was sent coastwise down the Mersey, past Wales,
round Land's End, up the English Channel and down
the Thames. The price to the farmer was not high
but cheese was a 'cash crop' and paid the rent.

In 1816 the London market was overstocked with
cheese, the price fell and it was difficult to make a
sale. Henry Tomlinson, steward of several large estates in Cheshire, approached the London factors in
an effort to get the season's cheese sold but was unsuccessful. Cheese was accumulating on the farms and
the rents could not be paid. Tomlinson turned his
attention to Manchester. Here, he found buyers,

provision merchants who supplied Manchester and other industrial towns in Lancashire and Cheshire. From this time onward the bulk of Cheshire cheese was sold in these northern districts. The markets attracted food from an ever-widening area; cattle from Scotland and sheep from the Lake District were driven along the roads to be slaughtered in Lancashire; corn came from East Anglia and the Midlands; butter, which does not keep as well as cheese, came mainly from Derbyshire or north Staffordshire; bacon was imported from Ireland.

A similar development took place around other centres of growing industrialization. Farms which had been carved out of the ancient Forest of Arden fed the ironworkers in Birmingham and the Black Country. The Plain of York, the Yorkshire Pennines and Wolds provided the woollen workers of the West Riding with beef, mutton and oats for the oatcakes which were the staple diet of the north of England. London, where the population was well over a million and increasing rapidly, drew food from the home counties and from counties far more distant. Turkeys and chickens from Norfolk were sold in the huge poultry market; cattle and sheep from the Cheviots came in droves to Smithfield, the largest cattle market in the country. More and more food was required and more was grown.

The increase in agricultural production was made possible by several changes in the farming world. It will be remembered that the introduction of turnips into the crop rotation allowed a larger number of cattle to be bred. Pastures were improved to support the increased herds. Breeding from selected cattle and sheep improved quality and increased size. These and other similar improvements in farming practice were pure gain. Other changes, though undoubtedly increasing the produce from the land, had bad social consequences for some classes of the farming community. This has previously been noticed and will be further explained later.

Some of the increased production, it is difficult to estimate how much, came from new farms formed from waste land or common. In the late eighteenth century it was calculated that there were more than 6 million acres of waste land in England out of a total of about 22 million. Some waste land was so poor that it could not be cultivated with advantage; some of it was worth improving if the demand for food was high; some could be made into fertile and profitable farms: during the industrial revolution thousands of acres of the last two types were enclosed. Sometimes the landowners of the village would divide the waste into sections, each taking his share and so enlarging his original holding. Sometimes new farms would be created. Enclosure of the waste was often done by private agreement, especially in districts where individual farms were the rule, or it would be done by Act of Parliament.

Before enclosure, waste land or common had been used in a number of ways, not very valuable in themselves but useful to the poorer villagers. Either by right or by custom they could use it for grazing a horse, cow or a few geese; they could gather wood or cut peat for fuel. Often small cottages, little more than huts, had been built and a garden or paddock surrounded with a hedge or wall. This was called squatting on the waste. The following extract from a Dorsetshire dialect poem illustrates the country-man's feeling about the uncultivated land that sur-rounded his village:

> Why, 'tis a handy thing
> To have a bit of common, I do know,
> To put a little cow upon in spring,
> The while one's bit of orchard grass do grow.
> Our geese run out among the emmet hills
> And then, when we do pluck 'em, we do get
> For sale some feathers and some quills;
> And in the winter we do fat 'em well
> And carry 'em to market for to sell
> To gentlefolks.
> And then, when I have nothing else to do
> Why, I can take my hook and gloves and go
> To cut a lot of furze and briars
> For heating ovens and for lighting fires.
> And when the children are too young to earn
> A penny, they can go out in sunny weather,
> And run about and get together
> A bag of cow-dung for to burn.

When the waste or common was enclosed, squat-ters and villagers who could prove a legal right received a small portion of land in compensation, but many could not prove their right—their only claim was 'the custom of the village'. This was sometimes allowed if the custom had been established for more than twenty years but often the claim of the squatter was denied.

Arthur Young, Sir Frederick Eden, Sir John Sinclair and William Cobbett, men from different walks of life and with different attitudes, all travelled about the country making a special study of British agriculture. Though agreeing that enclosure was necessary and, indeed, urgent in order to increase the production of food, all believed that hardship was inflicted on the poor villager when he could no longer use the common. Arthur Young, for example, writing in 1801, claimed that the loss of 'keep' for a cow on the common often made all the difference between independence and having to take poor relief from the parish. Young quoted a commissioner of enclosure as saying, with sorrow, that in the hundred enclosures in which he had acted, 2,000 poor persons had been injured.

In general, the injured suffered silently or made only a feeble protest; poverty and lack of education added to the fear of withstanding the richer and more powerful landowners kept them helpless though not always docile. John Fenna of Croxton, together with other villagers, gave the commissioners much trouble at the parish meeting. They had, it was recorded, 'disputed their claims with much vehemence'. They were requested to put their claims in writing. Fenna probably spoke for many of them when he said, 'I never was any use at making anything out.'

On the other hand, the enclosure of Otmoor, near Oxford, provoked an outbreak of violence. In 1813, a thousand men, women and children, armed with hatchets and bill-hooks, marched round the enclosed moor, destroying the newly erected fences. 'Sixty or seventy of them were seized and forty-four were sent off to Oxford in wagons.' They were rescued by a mob of townsmen shouting, 'Otmoor for ever.' Nevertheless, Otmoor enclosure was enforced although protests continued to give the authorities trouble for fifteen years.

Some enclosures were of benefit to men in humble circumstances, providing land which, without much outlay except hard work, could be improved into a farm. Lord Derby's steward had many requests from labouring men for permission to 'take in' land on the slopes of his grouse moors. Some of the letters are well written but some are obviously the work of a hand not used to writing. Isaac Moss asked for a lease of thirty acres. 'All that is improvable, I will improve,' he wrote. 'I design to build a house on it next summer and, please God, I will make such an improvement that neither you nor none of Lord Derby's stewards shall find fault with.'

Thomas Plant asked for twenty acres of waste. 'It was', wrote the steward, 'no manner of service' to Lord Derby and had always been thought worthless.

Plant was a capable man with 'power and judgment'. Plant waited for three years before he got his lease. He then built a house and made a farm which has supported a family for nearly 200 years and still does so. All over the country, on the hills of Dartmoor, Somerset and the Pennines and on scrubland between the villages of the Midlands, such farms were created by labouring men. They had initiative and energy in plenty but not much capital or education. 'Send me the lease that I can get it read at Leek' at the fair, wrote James Slack from Staffordshire, in a large childish print. Slack had obtained permission to 'improve 30 acres of waste' and also to get coal from an outcrop. The coal soon gave out but Slack continued on his farm and his son inherited it.

Enclosure of the open fields took a very different and more drastic course from the piecemeal enclosure of waste and common described above. An Act of Parliament must first be obtained and it was seldom that all the open-field farmers were in agreement on the advisability of enclosure. Meetings were held, a vote taken and the matter decided by the majority in 'size and number'. This meant that the larger landowners, even though fewer, could outvote the smaller landowners. Generally speaking, the larger landowners supported enclosure. They could afford the expense and were anxious to get their land into a compact block instead of scattered about the open fields. In a compact block, land could be divided into conveniently shaped and sized fields. It could be cultivated as the farmer wished without having to consider the ancient open-field regulations, which hampered the progressive farmer in making improvements.

After the Act was passed, commissioners, generally two in number, surveyed the village and made a list of the number of strips owned by each farmer and their acreage. Blocks of land were then allocated to each landholder which corresponded as far as possible to the amount and value of the strips previously held. For example, if a villager had had thirty scattered strips of one acre each, he now had thirty acres in a block. The pasture and waste was also divided and an amount of land equivalent to the number of cattle pastured was added to the block. The villager with a thirty-acre strip would generally have exchanged them for a forty- or fifty-acre farm. This would be a reasonable holding for a family farm.

The larger landowners would have had many more strips than thirty. Their new block farms would, therefore, be large—several hundred acres. They were divided into square fields, generally of five to ten acres, fenced and a new farm-house built in a convenient place for working the land. These new farms were sometimes worked by the landowner-farmer or by a bailiff, but many of them were let; tenant farmers increased in number during and after the period of enclosure. Creating large block farms was expensive but rents were charged accordingly. Rents rose to about double in the early nineteenth century.

The large square fields gave rise to a new term, spoken with pride, 'broad acres', in contrast to the narrow strips which they had replaced.

Unless there were special circumstances, such as market gardening, a holding of less than twenty acres hardly provided a bare living. In most villages they were in the majority. The small holders, many of whom had only one or two acres had managed by having an additional source of income, a by-industry —spinning, weaving, hat- or glove-making or they had worked on the larger farms when extra labour was needed. Unfortunately, it was this class which found it the most difficult to pay the cost of enclosure and the subsequent fencing, which together might reach £10 an acre. Moreover, at the time when the tide of enclosure was running swiftly, many by-industries were dying as the result of the factory system and additional sources of income of this kind were harder to get.

A fenced or walled enclosure of a few acres was not the equivalent of a strip in the open field and rights on the common. The small-holder could not, at the same time, grow a little corn, pasture a horse or cow and sheep within it nor could he gather firewood or cut peat. He could grow vegetables and keep a pig and sometimes this is what he did, earning his main living by working for wages.

Numbers of these small-holdings were sold; it is impossible to say how many or in what proportion to those that were kept. Writers at the time remarked on this aspect of enclosure and differing views were expressed. Some, for example Arthur Young and Cobbett, deplored the lot of the smallholder as being nearly as unfortunate as that of the cottagers who lost their rights on the waste. Others were of the opinion that he was better with a job and a wage than ekeing out a living on a tiny piece of land and wasting time watching a cow or a flock of geese on a common. It is certain that many small landowners sold their tiny allotments, became farm labourers or went to the towns and worked in the factories. Some stayed in the village and, unable to maintain themselves and their families, were forced to apply to the parish for relief. Their small allotments were bought either to be added to adjacent farms or to be thrown together to make a new farm of reasonable size.

Gradually, but with increasing speed towards the end of the eighteenth century, individual farms replaced open fields. By 1830, the agricultural landscape had become much as it is today—homesteads surrounded by fenced or walled fields. Farming organization was more in unison all over the kingdom; the ancient sharp division between 'open' and 'closed' districts had gone. The pattern that emerged during the industrial revolution remained unaltered for over a hundred years and much of it still remains.

The farming community could be divided into four social classes: landlords with an estate or estates of several farms which were let or leased, the owner-occupier who farmed his own land, the tenant farmer who rented his land and the farm-worker who earned a wage. This class structure has remained throughout until the present time though the number and proportion of each class has varied from time to time.

Landlords ranged from noblemen with thousands of acres in several different counties to country gentlemen with estates of half a dozen farms or less. Many of them had enlarged and improved their estates as the result of enclosure. They took a pride in managing them well, not only because it paid to do so but because to be known as 'an improving landlord' won esteem and approbation. Agriculture and its concerns were very much discussed in Parliament and in the press during the industrial revolution. Enthusiasm was aroused by its progress. The king, George III, was proud to be nicknamed 'Farmer George' and the new methods of agriculture were practised at Windsor.

The best landlords replaced the old thatched, wattle and daub houses and cottages with new ones made of brick with slated roofs. They laid drains to rid the land of surface water. They encouraged their tenants to adopt better methods of farming practice by including clauses in leases which insisted on the plentiful use of manure and the rotation of crops. Among the estate owners of the kingdom, many famous names are associated with agricultural progress. The Duke of Westminster drained 500 acres on his land at Eaton. He bought one million tiles a year for five years to construct 190 miles of drains.

The Duke of Devonshire built a model village for his estate workers. The fifth Duke of Bedford was the first president of the Smithfield Club, formed with the object of improving livestock, and he was also a member of the original Board of Agriculture. His brother, the sixth Duke, followed his example in holding 'Agricultural Fêtes' at Woburn, the family seat and he became president of the Royal Agricultural Society.

The first Earl of Leicester, Thomas William Coke (pronounced Cook) was an outstanding figure in the agricultural world of the eighteenth century. He was born in 1752 and his life more than spanned the period of the industrial revolution for he lived for ninety years. The family estate lay along the Norfolk coast at Holkham with, as he used to say, the King of Denmark across the North Sea as his nearest neighbour. The soil was poor and sandy and had been badly farmed. Improvements had been commenced by the previous earl who had also built an enormous and impressive mansion in Palladian style. When Coke succeeded to the estate at the age of 22, a few half-starved cows were the only livestock; no crops were grown except a scanty yield of rye. The rents from the estate totalled about £2,000 a year.

Coke had been educated at Eton and had travelled in Europe. He was tall, slender and exceptionally good-looking. His portrait by Gainsborough shows a face of almost womanly beauty. He was a crack shot, an excellent horseman and fond of outdoor sports. He was gay and attractive and it is said that when he was in Rome many women fell in love with him, including the wife of 'Bonny Prince Charlie', the Young Pretender to the Throne of England. He had landed estates in several counties and much wealth from other sources. He was M.P. for Norfolk. It seemed unlikely that he would take an interest in the unrewarding estate at Holkham.

However, the Whig party which he supported was in opposition to the Tory Government so Coke had no hope of gaining office. As we have seen, in aristocratic circles an enthusiasm for agriculture was fashionable. On one of his visits to Holkham his steward consulted him about the renewal of two farm leases. The rents were very low—3s. 6d. per acre—but the tenants refused to agree to an increase on account of the poverty of the soil. Coke decided to manage the two farms himself. From that time, 1778, until his death he devoted himself to improving the estate, setting an example to his tenants and stimulating them by the results of his own excellent management. He created 3,000 acres of fertile wheatland from the thin poor soil by heavily stocking it with cattle and sheep which were given additional food such as oil-cake. This enriched the manure from the animals and so enriched the soil. He also used bone manure obtained from the pieces rejected by the Sheffield cutlers as not good enough for knife-handles. This supplied nitrogen, in which the soil was deficient.

Coke followed 'Turnip Townshend' in including

turnips in a four-crop rotation. He set himself to improve his livestock by more and better food and selective breeding. His cattle, sheep and pigs became famous, not only in Britain but also in Europe and America. He was tireless in encouraging, advising and helping his tenants. Wearing the smock-frock of the farm-worker, he went the round of his estate explaining the different qualities of the various grasses for pasture and meadow, instructing in herd-management, persuading the reluctant and traditionally conservative farmers to grow turnips to 'rest' the ground after corn and often giving a demonstration himself of the way in which certain operations were best done. His farm buildings, houses and cottages were models; they cost him, over the years of his farming life, more than half a million pounds.

Within thirty years the annual rental of the Holkham estate had risen from the original £2,000 to £20,000. His tenants were able to pay this increased rent and also increase their profits. Coke gave them security by granting long leases, built a school for their children and helped them over years of bad harvests. Slow to accept new ideas and hostile at first, his tenants came to see the advantage of his methods. He was much loved. William Cobbett who, as the radical son of a farm labourer, had no great affection for landlords, said of Coke, 'Everyone (on his estate) made use of the expressions towards him which affectionate children use towards their parents.' His favourite saying was 'Live and let live.'

When he took over the estate, Coke knew very little about farming so he invited farmers and land-owners from neighbouring districts to Holkham to go over his farms, discuss problems with him and suggest improvements. This was the beginning of annual gatherings at the time of sheep-shearing which were attended by thousands of people from all walks of life. He had become a teacher as well as a learner. In 1818, 600 persons were entertained at Holkham Hall for a week. In the mornings they were taken round the estate; the evenings were spent in discussing what they had seen. The gay young man had become the 'unchallenged head of a little king-dom, contented and prosperous'. He was nicknamed, 'King Tom'.

One of Coke's most likeable characteristics was his desire to give other people the benefit of his know-ledge. He wished to see all British agriculture farmed in an enlightened way and thriving as at Holkham. Although many landowners and farmers followed the same course as Coke, though not often to the same extent, the spread of his new methods was very slow and uneven. Coke himself said that his im-provements travelled at the rate of ten miles in ten years. Well-farmed estates were often oases sur-rounded by estates which were much as they had been for centuries. Lord Shaftesbury came into the family estate in 1851, nine years after Coke's long life of constant improvement had ended. Shaftesbury found the land waterlogged, the farms ill managed

N   183

and unproductive, the houses and cottages 'filthy, close, indecent, unwholesome'. He longed earnestly to rebuild, drain and introduce new methods but rents were low and he had no capital.

'Oh! if instead of £100,000 to pay in debt, I had that sum to expend, what good I might do,' he wrote and his wish might have been echoed by many landowners. Shaftesbury's shortage of ready money was not his fault but many estates remained unimproved because of heavy mortgages to pay gambling debts or because their owners thought only of drawing rents. Nevertheless, good estate management by land-owners increased throughout the period of the industrial revolution. The indifferent landowner was much less common in the later nineteenth century. The gap between the best and worst practice was narrowed. In general, land became more valuable and rents increased.

The owner-occupier who farmed his own land and the tenant farmer might farm 500 acres or more or might have a small-holding of 30 acres or less. He might be a hill flockmaster with sheep grazing on a mountain and a few acres of meadow or arable. He might be raising vegetables and fruit for a town market on fertile land. He might practise mixed farming on newly enclosed land or he might have a dairy farm and produce milk, cheese and butter.

During the industrial revolution there were several periods when trade was bad and finance dislocated. Between 1795 and 1814 there was a run of rainy summers when the corn rotted and turned black in the fields and could not be harvested. Only twice were harvests abundant. In the same years, Britain was at war with France and it was difficult to import corn. The price of corn rose steeply from 52s. a quarter to the famine price of 119s., fell to 58s. and rose to 126s. in 1812. When the war was over, corn prices slumped heavily and remained low for many years. Under these circumstances farming was a gamble; money was both made, lost and made again.

In corn-growing districts the owner-occupier was rather better placed than the tenant farmer for the tenant farmer had to pay his rent in both good and bad years, though sometimes the rent would be reduced. In the very bad years of the 1820s many farmers ceased to grow corn and their farms 'tumbled down to grass'—poor grass for pasturing beasts. Many were bankrupt and gave up farming. Farmers raising cattle, horses and sheep and dairy farmers suffered from fewer ups and downs, especially if they were near to the growing industrial areas. Except for the difficulty of making hay in a wet season, they were not so dependent on the weather as corn farmers and, as we have seen, the rising population created new markets for their produce. Thus, there was no over-all prosperity for the whole period of the industrial revolution. Most farmers did well during the earlier half; some farmers had serious losses during the later half; some abandoned farming; some prospered throughout the period.

Robert Bakewell farmed through the earlier half of the industrial revolution. He died in 1795 at the age of 70. He inherited his father's grazing farm in East Anglia when he was only 20 years old. Bakewell was the pioneer of the method of improving livestock by selective breeding. He was a 'tall, broad-shouldered, stout man of red-brown hair and complexion, clad in a loose brown coat, scarlet waistcoat, leather breeches and top-boots', something like the 'John Bull' of cartoons. He concentrated on breeding sheep and cattle that would fatten quickly and provide larger and better joints. Under his hands the breed of scrawny, long-legged sheep, with large head and stringy flesh was transformed. Bakewell produced compact animals that cut up into tender, juicy chops, legs and shoulders. 'Small in size and great in value' was his motto.

Beef cattle also underwent a transformation but, though he tried over a number of years to improve the milch cow, in this he failed. Cows specialized for yielding large quantities of milk were not evolved until long after Bakewell's time. Indeed, it was found that breeding for beef actually reduced the breed's capacity for milk. Farmers who required an animal that would produce both milk and beef did not favour Bakewell's cattle. His sheep also had a disadvantage; their wool was less fine than that of the unimproved breeds. British wool manufacturers had to import fine wool from Spain to mix with the new coarse product and this was difficult and expensive when the country was at war. The discoveries of Captain Cook, which led to the settlement of Australia, provided a new provenance for wool and mutton. Flocks of sheep were sent to that country from Britain and were specialized for the two different uses.

Bakewell's horses were highly valued and became famous. Until Bakewell took them in hand, horses were mainly bred to be ridden or for use as pack-horses, carrying goods slung across their backs or in side baskets. Oxen were generally used for drawing carts or ploughing, though the use of the horse for these purposes was increasing. Turnpike roads and the growing volume of goods carried along them created a need for a draught animal that would be stronger than the riding-horse and faster than the ox.

Bakewell bred horses specially adapted for drawing heavily loaded carts and wagons. His black stallion, named K, was described enthusiastically as 'The grandeur and symmetry of form'. Bakewell's horses were eagerly sought by London dealers; they proved their worth in drawing huge brewers' drays and coal-wagons. Using Bakewell's methods other breeders produced horses suitable for many different kinds of work. Throughout the industrial revolution and until recently, the horse with loaded cart or wagon, the milkman's horse, the horse and trap and the carriage-horse were a familiar sight about the towns and on the highways.

Unlike Coke, who made every effort to get his ideas generally accepted, Bakewell was very secretive. When visitors came to his farm they marvelled at his livestock but he would not tell them of the way in which he got his results. It is said that, when his sheep were too old to breed from and were fattened for sale, he infected them with foot-rot so that no one could use them for breeding. In spite of all his precautions, however, his methods became known and were imitated. He was a keen man of business and made a lot of money. The price for the use of his rams rose from 17s. 6d. for the season to 20 guineas. Towards the end of his life he made over £3,000 a year from that source alone.

Bakewell did not alter his style of living as he became well-to-do. He retained the habits of the working farmer: early rising, dinner at noon and early to bed. At half past ten o'clock 'let who would be there he knocked out his last pipe' and retired. His kitchen was hung about with the skeletons and pickled joints of his most celebrated animals and surrounded by these grisly remains he lived and entertained. Many sightseers came to Dishley Farm as well as buyers, peers of the realm, royal dukes from France and Germany and a prince from Russia. He fed them in the kitchen on Dishley beef and mutton. He did not marry. As he grew older the crowds of people who visited him were still entertained with lavish hospitality. Like Chaucer's earlier English yeoman, 'It snowed meat and drink in his house.' This cost him more than even his considerable income could stand and it is reported that he died in poverty.

Bakewell was an unusual example of the owner-occupier-farmer. Thomas Furber was much more typical of this class and, since he rented land in addition to owning a farm, he can also be taken as an example of the tenant-farmer. He was born in the early years of the 1740s on a farm in the south of Cheshire which had belonged to his ancestors for over 200 years. In 1767, he married and commenced farming on his own account at College Fields, a farm of about 180 acres for which he paid £100 yearly rent. On his father's death in 1800 he moved to the family holding, Austerson Hall Farm, which was about twice the size of College Fields. He lived there until his death in 1820.

Over his fifty-three years of farming he kept careful accounts of his expenditure and sales. He did not make much profit at College Fields but the family lived mainly on the produce of the farm and Furber gradually built up his stock of cattle. At Austerson he made a handsome annual profit.

When Furber married he spent £25 on furnishing his farm-house. He bought one bed, '6 cheres, a childe chear and 2 armes chear'. He also bought chests and coffers, a frying-pan and 'saspan', a number of dishes and two spinning-wheels. He bought 44 lb. of wool which was made into blankets; his wife probably provided sheets. A warming-pan for airing the bed and a fruit-dish seem to have been the only extravagances. For stock he had 20 cows and a bull, 2 horses, 15 sheep, 2 pigs and 2 pigins (little pigs). Furber had no machinery so, apart from his plough, harrows and grindstone, all the work of the farm was done with tools—rakes, mattocks, spades, axes.

Cheese was the mainstay of the economy; the dairy was well stocked with tubs, presses and barrels. At College Fields, Mrs. Furber had two or three maids to help her in the house and dairy and there were one or two men for farm-work. At Austerson the number increased. All the help lived in the house. They were hired in January for a year and were paid at the end of the twelve months. Furber advanced small sums from time to time. 'Martha', for example, was hired for £2 7s. 6d. In the course of the year she was given 3s. to buy a pair of shoes, 3s. for cloth to make a 'shift', 9s. for a greatcoat, 2s. for stockings and small sums for other items. Martha suffered from toothache; 6d. was charged to her for a pain-killer. At the end of the year she had nothing to draw but Furber gave her 2s. 1d. 'above her wages'.

A few of Furber's farm-servants left at the end of the first year but most of them stayed on, sometimes for a number of years. Charles, who was hired in 1797, stayed for four years and his wages were advanced from £7 to £10, plus, as with all the other servants, board and lodgings. He never had more than a few shillings to draw—'Paid him at Crismas 5/11', wrote Furber in settlement of Charles's account. Most of the farm-servants' 'subs' were for clothing but Enoch, for many years the head man, had an occasional day off to go to Nantwich races or one of the local 'wakes'. Furber advanced him about £2 in most years for these jollifications. Enoch was the ploughman and was paid more than the other servants. He had a farm cottage but took his meals in the farm kitchen. Furber supplied him with a load of coal occasionally. He would presumably have a wife and children who would also work on the farm.

Two or three of Furber's farm-workers left before their term was completed. Of Soloman, Furber wrote, 'He over run me and went away, he come again but not hired.' Mary, who ran away in July, had been given money to buy a 'petticote', a bonnet, a pair of stays and 'when her head gathered'. There was about £1 owing to her but 'She left in the night' Furber recorded. The number of farm-workers was much greater than it would be today because of the absence of machinery. Besides managing the farm, Furber worked with his men and Mrs. Furber ran the dairy. Many hundredweights of cheese were produced in the summer season, forty cows were milked twice a day at Austerson, pigs were bred and raised, oats and barley grown and harvested. Furber's farms were not far from the Potteries. He was well placed for marketing his produce. It is evident from his accounts that he was a capable man for, though they are ill-spelt, they were carefully kept and show a steady increase in income.

Farm-servants who lived in the farm-house were in a much more secure position than the day-labourer. They did not suffer from unemployment during their term of hiring and the rise in the cost of living during the war years did not affect them. The day-labourer suffered acutely from both. Numerically, the day-labourer increased during the period of the industrial revolution for the new type of farming needed much more labour, particularly in hand-work such as weeding and hoeing. As a class they benefited little, if at all, from the improvements in agriculture and industry that brought wealth to others. They were considered to be almost the lowest of the social classes. As a class, they were helpless for they had neither parliamentary votes nor a voice in local government. When, in 1834, the field-labourers of Hampshire and Dorset tried to form trade unions, the government acted against them; their leaders were convicted of conspiracy and were transported as prisoners to Australia.

The day-labourer's wage rose from about 5 to 6s. a week to between 8 to 10s. during the period of the industrial revolution. Prices also rose and, on balance, the labourer could buy a tiny fraction more with his wages in the nineteenth century than he could in the eighteenth. He was, however, more dependent on his wages than he had been previously for, as we have seen, some sources of income had been lost with enclosure and the factory system. The day-labourer could only just live on his wage when he was in full work and it was necessary for his wife to help out the family income and also his children as soon as they could toddle. It was impossible for him to save and this was known and accepted. In times of unemployment, sickness and old age, he received small sums of money or food from the parish poor-rate.

In many parishes poor relief was given with a certain amount of rough humanity. Sheets and blankets for childbirth, coal or wood during severe winters, extra comforts, such as port wine and milk, for the sick and aged are often found recorded in the accounts of the overseers of the poor. Children in poor-houses or foster-homes in country districts had a diet not inferior to any that could be provided by a day-labourer and often, perhaps generally, it was better than that very low standard. Milk, bread and porridge were the usual fare, with meat and vegetables on Sundays and at Christmas. A little tea would be provided for the women as a treat and an occasional pint of ale for the men.

Clothing was given when necessary—woollen or print dresses and a pinafore for the women and girls, jackets, trousers and shirts for the men and boys. All wore woollen stockings and heavy boots or, in the northern parishes, clogs. There are occasional entries of shawls and mittens for the aged both in poor-houses or on out-relief and an exasperated overseer recorded, 'Another handkerchief for Dolly Day.' The 'another' is underlined. Until the end of the eighteenth century the number of labourers and their families in poor-houses was small; out-relief was their general recourse through the distresses and hazards of their life.

During the hard times which followed the end of

the war with France (1815), half the labourers in many villages were either out of work or only working a few days a week. Out-relief was given on so wide a scale that the poor-rate rose steeply and became a serious burden on the parish. To recover some of the expenditure, labourers on relief were hired to the local farmers by the parish. The result was that wages for labourers not on out-relief fell to 3 or 4s. a week since the farmers could get labour for this rate from the parish and so were not prepared to pay more. Riots broke out in the villages and farmers' ricks were burnt. The corn-growing districts were most seriously affected. Many day-labourers left their homes and occupation and went to the industrial areas where work was to be had in the factories. Samuel Greg, you will remember, founded his village at Styal with destitute exiles such as these.

On dairy and pasture farms, especially if they were near to the new centres of industry, the situation was not so black. This type of farming did not require day-labour in such large gangs as arable farming— only one or two labourers would be employed. The parishes could support them when they were in distress without them becoming a serious burden. Moreover, as we have seen, dairy and pasture farming did not suffer to any extent from the post-war slump. The government received hundreds of petitions from arable farmers complaining about the condition of agriculture and asking for a remedy. Very few were received from dairy or pasture farmers.

Day-labourers' wages were higher near the industrial towns and, even so, it was difficult to get and keep labour. The day-labourer had no contract; he could leave his employer with only a day's notice, walk to the nearest factory and get a job without much difficulty. Arthur Young recorded the complaint of many northern farmers that this factor increased the price of labour by as much as 3s. a week. More than this, they said, was demanded during harvest-time.

During the period of the industrial revolution the potato, previously only eaten occasionally, became a staple article of diet. This vegetable required for its cultivation a great deal of hand labour at infrequent intervals during the growing season and at harvest. Gangs of men, women and children, many of them from Ireland, were used for this work. They were recruited by gang-masters who moved them about the country to meet the demand. They were wretchedly paid, housed in barns and shacks and paid off at the end of the season. Gangs were employed in general agriculture from the beginning of the nineteenth century but no public inquiry or regulation of the conditions of gang labour were made for fifty years. The Agricultural Gangs Act of 1867 and the Agricultural Children's Act of 1873 gave some little protection to women and children but, throughout the industrial revolution, farm-workers in general made what bargain they could with their employers unsupported by government or trade union.

8

The Fight for Reform

DURING the earlier period of the industrial revolution, the minds and activities of inventors, employers
and managers were intensely engaged in solving the
many problems that arose from the new processes of
manufacture. Technical difficulties in making the
machines work, the management of labour and the
organization of the sale of large quantities of goods
were their main concerns. It seems, as we look back,
that they were so obsessed with making and selling
that they had no regard for the personal and social
consequences of their actions. With few exceptions,
the industrialists did little to remedy the evils of child
labour, overcrowded and insanitary conditions in
workshop and town or long hours of drudgery in
airless factories. Again with few exceptions, those
who did provide better conditions were moved by
pity and benevolence; they objected to any interference by government in their businesses.

We have seen how this attitude was slowly broken
down in relation to children, young persons and
women in textile factories. In the second half of the

nineteenth century these classes received legal protection in other trades. Adult male workers were, however, still regarded as being able to look after themselves and so not in need of help from any government. Many working men either agreed with this view or, because the parliament of the time was largely in the hands of the aristocracy, did not imagine that it could be used for their benefit. Moreover the new industrial population was not, at first, politically minded—they were engaged in new tasks in unfamiliar surroundings and, like their employers, they hardly realized that problems were accumulating as by-products of these changes.

Even when the new industrial population tried to influence Parliament, it could only be done indirectly for only about 100,000 of the fourteen million people in England had votes and these votes were very unequally distributed. The House of Commons was made up of two members from each county who were elected by landowners whose land was worth 40s. a year or over. Certain towns, called boroughs, also sent two members. The right to vote in these towns varied considerably but, in most instances, was confined to a very few hundred people and occasionally to only a handful. This pattern of parliamentary representation had originated in the Middle Ages and was reasonably suitable for the way in which the population was distributed at that time. By the eighteenth century it had become most unjust.

Great manufacturing towns such as Manchester

and Birmingham had no Member of Parliament to represent them and their inhabitants had no votes though the small market town of Appleby and the still smaller fishing-village of Looe returned two Members. Other places, such as Sarum in Wiltshire and Castle Rising in Norfolk, once thriving boroughs with markets and guild industries, had dwindled away and reverted to farmland; they also returned two Members to Parliament. They were called 'Rotten Boroughs' because they had 'decayed'. Of the counties, tiny rural Rutlandshire and Lancashire alike had two M.P.s, although Lancashire far outstripped Rutland in population as well as in area.

Local government was also out of step with the times. The boroughs had old corporations composed of a small body of burgesses who were not elected by the inhabitants but who controlled the town by virtue of having certain ancient rights or privileges such as a holding in the town land or the possession of a hearth on which a pot could be boiled. In the latter instance, the voters were called 'pot wallopers'; to wallop meant to boil with a loud bubbling sound. Pot wallopers who had left the town would return once a year, build a hearth, make a fire and boil a pot in public in order to keep the right to vote in being. There were other out-of-date and absurd customs connected with local and national government which left new-comers in the growing towns without a voice in public affairs. There were, however, some towns, for example Preston and Westminster, where the right to vote was much wider and included most of the adult male inhabitants but such towns were very few.

'Reform' (a juster and more equal distribution of votes and constituencies) had been proposed several times during the eighteenth century but there was no great public demand until the effects of the industrial revolution began to be widely seen and felt. From about 1790, however, pressure for reform gathered strength; during the first thirty years of the nineteenth century, reform of Parliament became a burning question, particularly in the industrial districts. Many factors contributed to an awakening sense of the importance of politics to both working people and industrial employers. Three Acts of Parliament sparked off a continuous and enthusiastic campaign.

In 1799, a Combination Act was hurriedly passed by a Parliament terrified by the success of the French Revolution. The Act made all agreements between workmen for bettering their conditions illegal. It was aimed at preventing any action by working people that would increase their power and possibly lead to an overthrow of state and constitution such as had happened in France. Combinations or, as we would say, trade unions had been formed in factories, mines and workshops for, by standing together and speaking with one voice, a better bargain could be made with employers.

The first factory workers to so organize seem to have been the spinners who, in 1785, formed the

'Friendly Society of Cotton Spinners of Stockport.' This was, as the name implies, a local society. Many others followed but there was, as yet, no national organization. Indeed, many combinations were no more than groups in factories. Combinations fostered a sense of unity and common interest among industrial workers, sometimes gained concessions from employers and were a check on attempts to pay lower wages or impose longer hours.

The power behind the combination was the strike —a common decision to stop work. Even the threat of a strike could be very effective if employers had plenty of orders for their goods and preferred to meet the workers' demands rather than have production stopped. As it was impossible to strike without agreement, work-people were prevented by the Combination Act from using this power. The penalty for breaking the new law was up to three months' imprisonment. Many hundreds of men and some women were convicted and served sentences under the Combination Act. Many more, by threat of prosecution, made humble and public apologies for 'Combining against their masters' and promised not to do so in future. The following examples show how the Act restricted the work-people's bargaining power.

In 1816, twelve men and eleven women were brought before a Stockport magistrate, the Rector of the Parish Church, Prescott by name. They were weavers and, in the winter months, their employer had deducted 6d. a week from their wages to pay for candles to light their looms during the dark hours. He forgot to restore the 6d. during the summer months and attempted to take another 6d. off when winter came round again. The weavers naturally objected and agreed among themselves to stop work rather than pay the double reduction. They were charged with forming a Combination. The Rector sent them out into a yard to decide whether they would go back to work or go to prison. All refused to return unless the 6d. was restored and each was sentenced to one month's hard labour.

In London the compositors of *The Times* newspaper were sentenced to terms of imprisonment, varying from nine months to two years for forming a union. This the judge who sentenced them called 'a most wicked conspiracy'. In the winter of 1809, the Durham miners came out on strike against the conditions of their employment. So many men were arrested that the jail could not hold them and they were confined, under military supervision, in the Bishop of Durham's stables. In this instance, the threat of the law broke the men's resistance; a sympathetic local rector and the captain of militia negotiated terms between the mine-owners and mine-workers and the men went back to work.

It is true that unions continued to exist and that new ones were formed even under the threat of prosecution. It was a common practice for the masters to apply, or threaten to apply, to a magistrate for a summons against workers known to have formed a union and then to proceed no further in return for a signed statement asking for forgiveness and a promise to form no unions in future. This statement was published in the local newspapers:

> WE, the undersigned, do humbly make submission and acknowledge the impropriety of our proceedings and return thanks for the lenity we have experienced in the very serious prosecution that pended over us being withdrawn . . .
>
> Whereas upward of eighty Colliers and workmen of Poynton, Worth and Norbury Collieries, in Cheshire, on the 24th. of September last (1810), assembled together in a wood and there resolved upon demanding from their employers an advance of wages . . .' On the demand being refused, 'all the said colliers left their work at once and remained out of employment for nine weeks to the extreme inconvenience of the public and great damage to the Collieries. For this unlawful and dangerous conspiracy a prosecution was commenced against the Secretary and Delegates of the conspirators, to answer which the undersigned were . . . to appear at the ensuing Sessions at Chester but have since applied to the Masters to be forgiven and to be permitted to return to their employment like the rest of the workmen without alteration in wages or restriction demanded which the Masters have consented to comply with, upon condition of their signing a submission to be published in the Chester, Manchester and Derby papers. . . .

This declaration was signed by eleven men, eight of whom could not write and so made a cross on the paper. Such admissions were evidently made by unwilling men, desperately afraid of imprisonment and forced to make any terms they could get after the long spell without wages. The Act did not prevent combination entirely; it drove work-people to secrecy, rebellion, riot and sometimes to violence. It also brought home to them the importance of being represented in Parliament for, without this, their protests had little or no weight.

Petition after petition was sent to the House of Commons for the repeal of the Combination Act, for a Minimum Wage Act and for other measures that would have improved the lot of the working population. They were all rejected. In 1811, a delegate of the cotton weavers who had been unable to obtain a hearing, reported on his return from London, 'Had you possessed 70,000 votes for the election of Members to sit in the House, would your application have been treated with such indifference, not to say inattention? We believe not.' The industrial workers came to see the truth of this, and, from the early years of the nineteenth century, the movement for the reform of Parliament had increasing support from them.

The industrial employers were rather later in demanding political representation. Perhaps the first realization of the way in which a government controlled by landlords could be used against their interests came in 1815. The end of the long war with France had brought widespread and severe depression. During the war the price of corn had been extremely high and rents had risen accordingly. Immediately after the war a Corn Law was passed, forbidding the importation of wheat from abroad unless the price of home-grown wheat reached 80s. a quarter. Thus, home-grown wheat was protected from the foreign competition which would have lowered its cost.

Bread, made from several varieties of corn—wheat, oats, rye—was an important article of working-class diet and the cost of the loaf affected wages. If bread were dear wages were forced to rise; if bread were cheap, wages could be reduced. Faced by the necessity of having to pay increased wages in order that farmers and landlords could prosper, the industrial employers protested. As they had little representation in Parliament, their protests were unheeded. Three years after the passing of the Corn Laws, another measure was passed which affected the industrial employers, in particular the textile manufacturers. This was the Act of 1819, which has previously been described; it controlled the hours and conditions of labour for children in cotton factories. These two Acts brought the employers into the reform movement in increasing numbers.

Many people, who were neither industrial workers nor employers, worked for parliamentary reform. They were moved by good will and a sense of injustice. Major Cartwright, who had served in the Navy, spent the early years of his retirement in campaigns against slavery and other evils. When he was over 60 he threw himself into the movement for reform and spent the next twenty years of his long life in writing, organizing and chairing meetings for the cause. He was not an eloquent speaker but his plain common sense and his faithfulness to his principles earned him the nickname of 'Honest John'. Until his death at the age of 84, he 'stumped the country', travelling many hundreds of miles over vile roads to enhearten and encourage groups of reformers in isolated places. He died in 1824, before the success of the cause was achieved.

William Cobbett's comments on the effects of enclosure on the small farmer and farm-labourer have been previously mentioned. Cobbett was an ardent advocate of reform and his writings did much to inform the industrial workers about public affairs and stimulate their interest. He was born in 1762, the son of a farm-labourer. He enlisted in the Army and served for seven years in Nova Scotia, where he got into trouble with the authorities for agitating for better conditions for the common soldier. He was threatened with prosecution and fled to France. In 1800 he settled in London and earned a living writing for newspapers. He was now nearly 40 years of age, stout, burly and ruddy in complexion—still very much the countryman.

From this time until his death in 1835, he wrote a constant stream of articles and published pamphlets, newspapers and books on a wide variety of subjects. They ranged from economics and politics to 'Advice to a Young Man on Getting Married'. He had a simple yet trenchant style which was popular with working-people. It is said that when the mail coach bearing his periodical, *The Political Register*, reached the industrial towns, eager crowds tore the parcels open and read them in the street. Groups of men and women, unable to read themselves, listened to those who could. Cobbett's reports of the debates in the House of Commons, which he published regularly, brought home the importance of Parliament and the urgent need for reforming that and other institutions.

Francis Place and Sir Francis Burdett were close friends and both were associated with the London reformers. Francis Place was a master leather-breeches maker and tailor who, after early struggles with poverty, opened a shop in Charing Cross and prospered. He denounced the Combination Act and was the leading figure in securing its repeal in 1824. He was a master of political 'wire-pulling' and gained his end by influencing and managing those in authority.

He took an active part in the Westminster election of 1807, when Sir Francis Burdett stood as a candidate in favour of reform.

Westminster was one of the few constituencies where many working-people had the right to vote; it had an electorate of over 10,000. Francis Place, who wrote an account of the election, undertook the task of persuading and organizing the electors to vote for 'Burdett and Radical Reform'. Sir Francis was an educated and wealthy gentleman who had spoken strongly against flogging in the Army and Navy. He opposed the bribery and corruption of voters, a common practice at that time. He, himself, did not think that he would win the election. The majority of voters were poor and uneducated and not, he supposed, likely to vote from conviction or by persuasion without a cash payment.

The result of the election surprised him and the country generally. Sir Francis was elected by a large majority. In Parliament, he formed one of a tiny, but growing band of reformers. He was twice imprisoned for his activities during the campaign for reform, once in 1810 and again in 1820. There was a wide variation in the demands of the reformers. There were those who would have been content with the abolition of the 'rotten boroughs', together with the creation of new constituences in the manufacturing towns; at the other extreme there was a demand for complete adult suffrage, such as we have today. Sir Francis Burdett advocated 'universal suffrage' and moved a Bill to that effect in the House of Commons (1818). Later, his views became more moderate. He lived to see the first Reform Bill pass into law (1832) and this, though far from his original claims, contented him.

Samuel Bamford, another prominent worker for reform, came from a very different walk of life. He was a Lancashire silk weaver. He has left us an account of his life and of the reform movement among the industrial workers of the north. He was born in Middleton, a textile town in south Lancashire in 1788 and died in 1872 within a mile or two of his birth-place. His eighty-four years more than spanned the industrial revolution. He was moulded by it; no other time could have produced such a man. His father was a silk weaver and so was his wife. The weaving of silk was not generally mechanized until the second half of the nineteenth century—silk weavers were able to earn a decent living long after hand-loom cotton weavers had sunk into poverty. Sam was born and grew up in a relatively prosperous time for those of his trade. He was sent to school in Middleton, learned to read and write and, for a year or two, was a scholar at Manchester Grammar School. He learned a little Latin of which he was rather proud for he introduced Latin 'tags' from time to time in his writing.

In his early twenties he became the father of a child by a woman to whom he was not married. He was taken before a magistrate and ordered to pay 5s. a week towards the child's support. In his own words, 'In pleading guilty to that, I do it with shame and regret.' Sam paid the affiliation order regularly for seven years and, in the meantime, he married and set up in business for himself as a silk weaver. A daughter was born. Sam wrote of this child with the greatest affection. He was something of a poet and composed many verses expressive of the warm and tender bond which united the little family. His wife worked beside him at the loom, which stood in the 'house-place' of the four-roomed Middleton cottage.

Sam was an active reformer. He had been sent as a delegate from Middleton to a London conference, where he had met Sir Francis Burdett, Francis Place, Major Cartwright and other leading men in the movement. Sam wrote a lively account of this conference with character sketches of the people who attended it. Of Major Cartwright he wrote, 'Let me pause and render a tribute due to integrity and benevolence.' Of the others he did not think much. Sam was very cocksure in his judgments and rather touchy —in Middleton he was a well-known figure; among national leaders in London he was only one of a crowd and this he did not like. At this time he was about thirty years old, tall and lanky, Lancashire in speech, his features 'like a mass of rough and smooth, which, thrown into a heap had found their own subsistence, an intelligent eye and a rough good nature'. So Sam described himself. He had also considerable basic common sense.

Back from London, Sam became involved in the ill-fated Blanketeer movement. This was an attempt to carry a petition in favour of reform on foot to London. The men taking part had blankets strapped to their backs in which to sleep at night. The Blanketeers assembled in Manchester but were dispersed by police and yeomanry (armed volunteers, mounted on horses). Many were arrested. A few hundred got as far as Stockport where, on the bridge over the Mersey, again they were stopped with violence and haled off to prison. A remnant struggled as far as Macclesfield and met with the same treatment; two escaped and eventually reached London.

Sam at first approved of the project but soon saw that success was improbable because the date proposed, March 1816, did not allow enough time to organize and also because the weather likely to occur in that month would make walking and sleeping 'rough' uncomfortable. He spoke strongly against the march at the second meeting held to arrange it. Nevertheless, his name was included in a list of those present. This list was given to the Manchester magistrates by government spies, many of whom were stationed about the country, especially in the industrial districts. Sam, though he had done nothing illegal, was known as a reformer and a pretext was contrived for his arrest and disgrace.

During the slump in trade after Waterloo, Sam had been short of work and had got behind with the payments for his illegitimate child. For this he was arrested when coming out of church on a Sunday morning. He was imprisoned for four days, during which time his wife made arrangements to pay the amount owing (£2 19s.) by instalments. This she subsequently did. Sam returned to Middleton to find that a round-up by the local constables of those known to be in favour of reform was in force, making it unsafe for him to remain at home. The leading reformers went into hiding. Sam and a friend went by night over the moors towards Oldham where they hid in various farm-houses and inns. The whole district was sympathetic and they were fed and sheltered. Sam's companion, 'Dr.' Healey, was a herbalist who also did minor surgical operations and dentistry. He took the opportunity of pulling a few teeth *en route*.

After a while, thinking it would now be safe, the two returned home, only to be immediately arrested by the deputy constable of Manchester, Nadin. Nadin was accompanied by eight police officers armed with blunderbusses. Sam was handcuffed and his wife, who clung to him, was threatened with shooting. It was an ugly situation for a crowd had gathered at the door and stones were thrown at the police officers. Sam appealed to the crowd to refrain from violence and suggested that it would be more sensible if they warned the other reformers of what was happening. On his way to Manchester, standing handcuffed in a cart, Sam saw the country-side alive with fleeing people, 'running like hunters'. He pointed this out to Nadin and told him that he would not get any more reformers that day for word of the presence of the police had been passed round. The deputy constable 'growled out a deep oath and said that he had never seen anything like it before'. The repressive measures taken by the authorities were welding the industrial workers together and against the police.

Sam was taken to London in irons and charged with High Treason. He was examined and re-examined by the Home Secretary, Lord Sidmouth; after a month in prison he was bound over to keep the peace and discharged. The attempted march of the Blanketeers was one of many efforts to bring pressure on the government and rouse public opinion. From 1818 onward the reformers of Manchester and district concentrated on organizing a monster meeting to be held in St. Peter's Field, an open space in the centre of the town. A series of preliminary open-air meetings was held in the towns and villages in the area round Manchester. The meetings were broken up by yeo-manry and many arrests were made but still the organization went on.

Petitions for reform, on which there were many thousands of signatures, were collected. A national speaker, Henry Hunt, was engaged to address a series of meetings in the Midland towns on his way from London to culminate in the Manchester demonstra-tion. It was intended that Hunt, on his return, should take the petition to the House of Commons. The right to petition was legal but large croweds could become unruly and so incur the charge of 'riotous assembly'. Many reformers had been arrested on this charge. Sam Bamford pondered on this problem. What was the difference between a meeting and a mob? He wrote, 'We had frequently been taunted for our ragged, dirty appearance and at the confusion of our proceedings.' Cleanliness, sobriety, peace, order must be the order of the day.

Accordingly, in order that discipline might be instilled, evening after evening and Sunday after

Sunday, crowds of reformers met on the moors above the cotton towns where they were drilled by ex-sergeants from the Napoleonic wars. No weapons, not even sticks, were carried but, in the course of learning to form into lines and squares, a clap of the hands was substituted for firing. Spies reported this to the Home Office and alarm grew as to the outcome of the Manchester meeting.

Sam was in charge of the Middleton contingent and it is from his account that we know, among much other interesting detail, that women were present at the moorland rehearsals and also that they voted in committee with the men. Women were active in the movement for reform, especially in the section that advocated 'universal suffrage' for this included women's right to the vote as well as men's. Many towns had separate branches for women, 'The female Friends of Reform'. A hundred years were to pass before this aim was achieved. The presence of women at the drill instruction and the intention to include them and the children in the processions to the Manchester demonstration is strong evidence for the peaceful intentions of the reformers. Sam Bamford certainly took measures to avoid provocation; for the ten-mile walk from Middleton to Manchester he refused even walking-sticks to all but the old or crippled.

On Sunday evening, 15 August 1819, after addressing enthusiastic meetings at Leek and Macclesfield and receiving demonstrations of support from the

villages on his route, Henry Hunt arrived at Stockport. Thousands of reformers awaited him and the
townspeople were in a ferment of excitement. A
government spy, Lloyd, wrote to the Home Office,
'The lower orders are in a dreadful state, bold and
insulting. Reform will give them complete control
over us. We will have none of it.' Lloyd also sent
word to the Manchester magistrates that a huge
crowd could be expected in St. Peter's Field on the
following day and advised them to have sufficient
force in readiness.

Monday, August 16th, was a day of brilliant sun-
shine. A coach, provided by a local sympathizer, had
been lavishly decorated with red and white ribbons.
Seated in the coach and accompanied by two women,
wearing white dresses and 'the red cap of liberty',
Henry Hunt headed a procession of over 5,000 people.
They were dressed in their 'Sunday best'—men,
women and children and some babies in arms. To
the sound of music from a band and walking in fours,
the procession set off along the road to Manchester.

Similar processions of equal and even larger numbers were converging on St. Peter's Field—from Oldham, Ashton, Rochdale, from the industrial villages
of south Lancashire and north Cheshire and, led by
Sam Bamford, the Middleton contingent marched
smartly along. A platform had been erected in St.
Peter's Field. An immense crowd, 80,000 persons at
the lowest estimate, gathered round. Hunt, a popular
and fiery orator was greeted by a great burst of

cheering as he arrived. He mounted the platform and began to speak.

Meanwhile, the Manchester magistrates, alarmed by the reports of spies, amazed by the vast throng of people and fearful of riots should they become violent, were watching the meeting from the upper floor of a shop on the outskirts of the Field. They had stationed a body of yeomanry near by and had also requested help from the Army. Contingents of soldiers were in the town. Hearing the shouts of applause in response to Hunt's opening sentences the magistrates panicked and ordered the yeomanry to disperse the meeting. The yeomanry rode towards the platform at a gallop, flourishing their sabres. The crowd, terrified, pressed tighter together and closer to the platform and those in front were trampled to the ground. Unable to disperse the crowd, the yeomanry seem to have lost their heads; they used first the flat and then the edge of their sabres to cut their way through.

Hundreds of people were wounded, including 113 women; 11 people were killed, including 1 child and 2 women. Within a few minutes the scene resembled a battlefield, the ground strewn with the dead and wounded. Men and women fled in all directions and hid from the pursuing horsemen in the narrow streets and alleys that surrounded the Fields. Sam Bamford found refuge in a cellar, where he was sheltered and tended by a friendly woman who was sympathetic to the cause of reform. Towards evening, he ventured

P   215

out and made his way by back streets to the east of the town. Here he found the shocked and straggling remnants of the Middleton contingent. He gathered them together, formed them into line and, tattered banner aloft, he marched them singing down the long road back to Middleton market-place.

Henry Hunt and many others were arrested at the meeting. Other reformers, including Sam Bamford, were later arrested at their homes. They received sentences which varied between one and two and a half years; Sam's one-year sentence was served in Lincoln Castle jail. He was treated with great consideration by the friendly and humane governor. He had a room to himself and was allowed pen and paper. He used these to write an account of the Manchester meeting and its tragic conclusion, many letters to reformers, friends and family and a great deal of verse. The following was written to his wife and describes his arrest which took place in the middle of the night in order to prevent disturbance.

TO JEMINA

I never will forget thee, love
Tho in prison far I be.
I never will forget thee, love
And thou wilt still remember me.

Oh! they may bind but cannot break
This heart so fondly full of thee
That liveth only for thy sake
And the high cause of libertie.

216

They came at night and did surround
My humble dwelling while I slept
And I awoke and heard a sound
Of feet as if they softly crept.

Awake, my love, I softly said
Awake, the enemy is near
Come, kiss me, be thou not afraid,
A wife of mine should never fear.

Arise and dress yourself, my dear,
These fellows brook but short delays.
Here is your petticoat and here
Your kirtle, hankerchief and stays.
For me love, I can bide their gaze.

The attack on the crowd by the yeomanry at
Manchester in 1819 came to be called 'Peterloo'; the
name embodies the idea of Waterloo (a battle) and
the place where the meeting was held. Peterloo was
important because it greatly influenced the public
opinion of the time. Many other meetings had been
broken up with violence and had caused no stir, for
little was said or written about them. It so happened
that a *Times* reporter was present in Manchester over
the week-end and went to the meeting out of curio-
sity but not thinking it was likely to be of much
interest nationally. He was shocked at what he saw
and he reported it faithfully. Also, the Rector of
Alderley (afterwards a famous Bishop of Lincoln)

who had ridden on his cob into Manchester to see his lawyer, gave public testimony to the peaceful intentions of those who attended the meeting. He had overtaken groups of reformers and family parties who were making their way to St. Peter's Field and had had some conversation with them. The Rector was surprised at the enthusiasm for reform which had collected such large numbers of people together but he was in no doubt that their behaviour was legal and proper. He had joined the magistrates to watch the demonstration and very much deplored their action in ordering out the yeomanry.

The Times reporter and the Rector were independent witnesses to the facts and their words carried weight. Slowly the balance of public opinion, hostile or indifferent at first, veered towards sympathy with the reformers and, later, towards favour of reform itself but the industrial workers had been badly discouraged. Writing after Peterloo, Lloyd reported that 'they are quite done for at present, quite in the dumps'. In the decade that followed, agitation for reform was promoted and organized largely by the industrial middle classes in the new towns and in London. They were supported by a growing number of M.P.s in the House of Commons and by a small group in the House of Lords. The struggle for reform became respectable. Because of their wealth, education and experience in management, these reformers were better equipped to bring pressure on the government than the working-people had been.

George IV, who had been first Regent and then King of Great Britain for over thirty years, died in 1830. He had been bitterly opposed to the reform of Parliament in any degree. He was succeeded by William IV, who was favourable to a moderate change in the constitution. In the same year the Whig party, whose leaders now supported moderate reform, gained a majority in the House of Commons and formed a government. A Reform Bill was immediately introduced and, after being hotly debated for seven sittings of the House of Commons was narrowly defeated. The Government resigned and an election took place. The Bill provided for the sweeping away of 'rotten borough' representation and the creation of constituencies in forty-two new towns and districts, including Birmingham, Manchester, Leeds and Sheffield. County representation was enlarged. The right to vote was given to all town householders paying a yearly rental of £10 or over and was extended to include some leaseholders and tenants in the country.

Manual workers, farm-labourers and the lower-paid classes as a whole received no benefit and were bitterly disappointed. Nevertheless, with some exceptions, they supported the Bill as an immense step forward. The election which was fought solely on the Bill, aroused great popular enthusiasm and was conducted with excitement amounting to fury. The election slogan was 'The Bill, the whole Bill and nothing but the Bill.' A new Parliament was elected in which there was a large majority in favour of reform. A second Reform Bill was immediately passed by the House of Commons but was thrown out by the Lords. Public indignation reached a crescendo. Packed meetings were held all over the country, fierce riots broke out in Bristol and at Nottingham the castle was burned. A cry arose for the abolition of the House of Lords.

The hero of Waterloo, the aged Duke of Wellington, led the opposition. He was now 83 years old and he was all but stone deaf. He could neither be silenced nor answered for he could not hear arguments or interruptions. He talked on interminably. The industrialists threatened to withdraw their money from the Bank of England and so disrupt the country's finance—'To beat the Duke, go for gold', they cried and placards bearing this admonition were plastered up and down the country, especially in London. The windows of the Duke's London house were broken several times by angry mobs.

In the midst of the turmoil, William IV went down to the City and was (most unfairly) hissed by an angry crowd who also threw stones at the royal coach. The King returned, fuming, to St. James's Palace and declared that, unless the Lords passed the Bill, he was now prepared to create enough new peers to force the measure through. This proved not to be necessary. The threat was enough. Confronted by an overwhelming public opinion against them, Wellington and a hundred of his supporters abstained

from voting and, in 1832, after forty years of continuous effort and eighteen months of intense agitation, the Bill was passed and became the First Reform
Act.

9

An End and A Beginning

HISTORY is a continuous process; there are no true beginnings or ends. Present and future arise out of the past and are, in this sense, part of it. There must, however, be an end to a book. This last chapter can only indicate some links between the industrial revolution and what came after.

Many millions of people lived through the industrial revolution; those whose lives have been described are only a tiny sample. Large sections of the community were little affected at the time and would hardly notice what was happening or realize how important it was to be. There were, for example, at the beginning of the period over half a million women who were domestic servants. By 1850, their number had increased to over a million. In some large towns the introduction of piped water would ease the work of the servant-maid but this would be offset by smuts from the factory chimneys, which sullied clothing, curtains and furniture and needed constant toil to remove.

Cheap abundant cotton was poured out by the new

machines. The domestic servant could be provided with washable dresses, white caps and capacious aprons for housework and could buy a print frock for her day off duty. Otherwise her life was little altered. She laboured with the ancient tools of dustpan and broom, hauled coal from the cellar and carried slops and water up and down stairs, for even where piped water was available there was seldom a bathroom. The domestic servant could not know and would not imagine that the inventions of her time would ease the way for new inventions which, in time, would mechanize much of the drudgery of domestic work. That domestic servants are no longer commonly employed and that their pay and conditions have improved out of all recognition is a long-term result of the industrial revolution.

The industrial revolution made very little difference to the lives of the country gentry unless their estates were in or near to the manufacturing districts. If so, they might benefit by an increase in the value of their land. Some of them sold their estates and moved to more pleasant surroundings, not considering an industrial town a 'suitable home for a gentleman', to quote Omerod, a contemporary historian. Jane Austen was writing her excellent novels in the period; they are set in the rural areas of the south of England. None of her characters seems to be aware of the changes that were taking place. They move elegantly about their drawing-rooms, dine with their neighbours and pay an occasional visit to London or Bath much as had been done for several generations past.

There is an occasional slighting reference to a fortune 'made in trade' or a new-comer from Birmingham 'and not much can be expected from Birmingham, you know'. Her young ladies might now have a dress made of muslin from Manchester instead of India; Josiah Wedgwood's new china could grace the table and a pair of his 'classical' ornaments stand on the mantlepiece.

The craftsmen who built and furnished the halls and mansions of the wealthy continued in the traditional ways of their trade and so did the village craftsmen—carpenters, wainwrights, blacksmiths, shoemakers. All clothing was still sewn by hand though a knitting-machine had been invented that cut out much of the labour in making stockings. Many other ways of life remained unchanged for many decades but slowly the industrial revolution, in its later developments, made an increasing impact. Country gentlemen, craftsmen, seamstresses, servant-maids— the very words suggest an age past and seem inappropriate to the present—another long-term result of the industrial revolution.

A short-term result was the revolution in transport made possible by the adaption of Watt's steam-engine to locomotion. The tramway train drawn by an engine was in use for hauling coal from the early years of the nineteenth century. George Stephenson constructed his first engine in 1814 and in 1823 he was appointed engineer to the Stockton and Darlington Railway. The Liverpool and Manchester Railway for goods and passengers was opened in 1830. The full impact of this new and much more speedy method of transport was not felt until the middle of the nineteenth century, by which time the country had been covered with a network of railway lines and people had become accustomed to travel by train.

The fear of the effect on canals of 'those damned tramways', expressed by the Duke of Bridgewater was justified. Much larger loads could be carried by train at much greater speed. Carriage along canals dwindled until they were mainly restricted to imperishable goods that were not needed in a hurry. Passenger transport on canals vanished almost entirely. The canal folk, who had been such a feature of life during the industrial revolution, became fewer and fewer and those who were left found it more difficult to make a living. They tended to hang on to their job but, as the older ones died or dropped out, they were not replaced to the same extent by a younger generation of bargees. Nearly all the canals were purchased by the various railway companies. Under their management, some waterways continued to carry a reasonable but decreasing amount of traffic but many were almost completely disused.

Under the competition of railways, road transport altered in character. Long hauls of heavy goods in wagons, long-distance stage-coach passenger service and horse-back riding on extensive journeys were gradually discontinued. They were replaced by the goods and passenger train and the 'express'. There was, however, an increase in short-haul horse traffic. Lorries took goods from the stations and goods yards and distributed them locally. Cabs and private carriages waited at the stations to convey passengers to their local destinations. The habit grew of living out of town and near to a station; business men either walked or were driven to and from it to their homes. The whole apparatus of long-distance road transport, turnpikes, toll-houses, coaching-inns where lodgings, food, drink and stabling could be obtained, became unnecessary and fell out of use. Until the coming of the motor car, country roads and inns, formerly so busy, were comparatively deserted. Passengers needing accommodation stayed at the new Station Hotel.

During the industrial revolution the advantages to be gained by a widespread system of education for the mass of the people were realized, but only slowly. Many grammar schools had been endowed in previous centuries until, in the eighteenth century, most towns and some villages had a school of this description. School with simpler aims, where reading, writing and cyphering were taught had also been established by charitable persons and it seems that the number of people who were literate was not inconsiderable at the onset of the industrial revolution.

The rapid increase in population and the difference in the way it was distributed made this provision quite inadequate and the number and proportion of people unable to read or write increased. Moreover,

226

as firms grew larger and industry more complicated, there was a greater need for clerks, store-keepers, book-keepers and accountants. Literacy was an advantage also in other and more humble jobs not, it was felt, necessary for the labourer or mill-hand but useful in, say, a messenger. Advertisements of such posts in contemporary newspapers add to the qualifications required (honesty and sobriety), 'Should be able to read.'

The first provision of education for the new industrial workers came from religious bodies or benevolent persons acting from a religious motive. It was thought that vice, crime and disorderly conduct among the 'lower orders' were due to the lack o. religious instruction and inability to read the Bible. Schools, held on Sunday, were opened in industria and mining districts to teach reading coupled with scripture lessons. There was some doubt at first of the advisability of teaching the poor to write but, later, this was conceded. Sunday schools were popular and, in the 1780s it was estimated that over half a million adults and children had attended them at one time or another. The teachers were not trained or paid. Not much could be learned in the few hours of teaching but all agreed that children attending a Sunday school improved in manners, behaviour and cleanliness (washed hands and tidy hair and clothes were required).

The Factory Acts of 1801 and 1819, which have previously been described, enacted that children in

227

factories should be taught reading, writing and arithmetic. Some employers like Samuel Greg and Robert Owen provided good schools and teachers but generally the provision was very poor. The following description is taken from the autobiography of Thomas Wood. 'I well remember the school at Bingley. It was a cottage at the entrance to the mill yard. The teacher was a poor old man who had done odd jobs of a simple kind for about 1s. a week. Lest he should teach too much or be too costly, he had to stamp washers out of cloth with a heavy wooden mallet on a large block of wood during school hours. No time-table said for how long.' Loud constant banging would not help towards the concentration necessary for learning.

Apart from the question of cost, one of the greatest difficulties in extending education to the children of poor parents was the shortage of teachers. In the early years of the nineteenth century a system of 'mutual instruction' was adopted. Classes were divided into small groups, each in charge of a monitor. Monitors were selected from the more able children. They received from the teacher some short piece of information, such as a list of dates, 'the rivers of England', 'capes and bays' or a multiplication-table, learned it by heart and taught it to the group. A great deal of factual material could be taught in this way with few teachers and small expense. Numbers of schools, based on this system, were opened by the Church of England and by the Nonconformist churches. The schools were supported by voluntary subscriptions supplemented by fees from the pupils. When these could not be afforded, they would sometimes be paid by charitable persons.

So far we have been dealing with education for the poor which, as can be seen, was provided from funds voluntarily subscribed. For those who could pay the cost, there were private tutors and governesses, private day and boarding-schools of varying quality, some very expensive, some costing only a few coppers a week. Nowadays the idea of free education, paid for by rates and taxes is generally accepted but this has only been gained slowly and painfully. Public responsibility for education commenced with a small grant-in-aid. In 1833 the First Reformed Parliament granted £20,000 towards education and appointed a committee to administer the fund; the money was to be distributed among schools deemed to be worthy and in need of help. Even at that time, £20,000 was not much for all England either for the existing need or for expansion but it was a beginning.

The grants gradually increased and, as they increased, conditions were imposed concerning the standard of education taught. Government inspectors were appointed to see that public money was properly spent. Religious bodies were encouraged by grants to take scholars not belonging to their denomination. By many steps, slowly the government took more and more responsibility for education. From these small beginnings our present educational system developed. It is one of the most important results of the industrial revolution.

Following the excitement that accompanied the passing of the Reform Bill, a general election was held and, in 1833, a new Parliament met in which the new voters and new constituencies were represented. In the First Reformed Parliament and in many later ones, landowners were still present in force and there was scarcely a member of the Cabinet who was not a peer or an heir to a peerage. It is true that the industrial towns now had voices in the House of Commons. Manchester had returned two members, one of whom was Mark Philips, a successful Manchester merchant born in the town. William Cobbett, whose writings had done so much to rouse and inform public opinion, was elected at Oldham and reformers now sat for Birmingham and other constituencies. Industry and commerce were, therefore, represented but without the power of a majority.

Nevertheless, a decisive change had taken place. The course taken by government and Members of Parliament alike is greatly influenced by the people who elect them, by the 'feeling in the constituencies'. An M.P. or a government must consider the interests of voters or they risk losing the next election. As the middle classes now had the vote, the parliaments that followed the Reform Act were responsive to pressure from them and many acts were passed which would not have been possible before.

A good example is the repeal of the Corn Laws. By

these laws, you will remember, the price of bread was controlled in the interests of farmers and landlords. Agricultural and industrial interests were directly opposed in this matter yet the industrialists were able to force the government to abolish the Corn Laws. They conducted a rousing campaign and organized the voters against M.P.s who opposed repeal.

The M.P.s who represented the industrial and commercial interests gradually increased in number and formed a new political party—the Liberals. The Liberals took the place of the older Whigs in opposition to the Tories. The Liberal Party became very strong, particularly in the industrial districts. Within thirty years of the Reform Act, Liberals were included in the government. Later, they were able to form governments themselves.

The reform of Parliament was followed by sweeping changes in local government. The Municipal Reform Act of 1835 abolished the old corporations and provided that all members of town councils should be elected by the ratepayers. Since this Act, town councils have been increasingly active in providing water, sanitation, street-paving, cleansing and lighting and many other amenities which are taken for granted today.

The idea of 'universal suffrage' not attained by the First Reform Act, was by no means abandoned. Agitation for a further extension of the right to vote was not entirely discontinued. Although discouraged and disheartened in the 1830s, the movement slowly gathered strength and rose to a crescendo in the 1840s. It was not, however, until 1867 that a Second Reform Bill was passed. This Act gave the vote to all householders in towns and extended the country vote. The town worker was now enfranchised and over a million voters were added to the electorate. Other Reform Bills followed; all were hotly contested. In 1930, a hundred years after the First Reform Act, with the granting of votes to women, complete adult suffrage was finally achieved. This is one of the most important long-term results of the industrial revolution, perhaps the most important. Government for the people is now also government by the people; they can, by using their votes, mould it to their will. This and much else we owe to the people who lived through the industrial revolution and it should not be forgotten.

APPENDIX I

Report of Committee on State of Children in Manufactories (Peel's Committee) 1816

EXTRACTS

John Sharron Ward, Bruton, Somersetshire, Silk Manufacturer;
'Children that frequent factories make almost the purse of the family. They share in the ruling and are in a great state of insubordination to their parents.'

Robert Owen, New Lanark, Cotton Manufacturer;

'The way in which many of these infants are first employed is to pick up the waste cotton from the floor, to go under the machines, where bigger people cannot creep and the smaller they are the more conveniently they can go under the machines.'

Sir Robert Peel, Ramsbottom, Cotton Manufacturer;

'At present, the hours allotted to the employment of children may be said to exceed their strength, but that being a peculiar business in which adults and children are employed promiscuously, we could not do justice to one without injury to the other.'

Report of Committee on Factory Children's Labour (Sadler's Committee), 1831

EXTRACTS

James Empson, Leeds, woollen weaver;
'The little boy here is my son. He is six years old last Christmas. I

233

sent him to work at the Albion Mill, Pudsey, about three weeks since. He was slubbing woollen yarn. He was to have no wages. He went to learn. On Friday night last the over-looker took the doffer strap 4″ wide and beat the boy as you can see.' (The boy was then undressed so that the bruises, black and red, could be seen covering his back, one arm and a shoulder.)

Mr. J. Walker of White Cloth Hall, Leeds;

'We have no particular rule regarding the age at which we admit children to the mill . . . but we find that the younger they come the greater the advantage derivable from their labour. They are more tractable, more quick and have greater facility in learning their work. We prefer them at seven years of age but we may occasionally take them a few months earlier.'

Report of Lords Committee on Chimney Sweep Boys

EXTRACTS

Evidence of a master sweep;

QUESTION: Have you ever known an instance of a boy sent up a chimney flue on fire.

ANSWER: Yes, and rejoiced I have been many a time, when such a job has come, to get sixpence for myself or a shilling; an active child will not let the fire rest on him; we pin the bosum of the shirt over, secure it in every way, so that the fire cannot get at him; we wet the brush and when one boy is tired, we send up another and, if he keeps in motion the fire will not lodge; if he is sluggish, he will be likely to be burnt.

APPENDIX II

Lower Withington, Cheshire,
Overseers of the Poor's Accounts, 1778–9

EXTRACTS

	£	s.	d.
Jno. Swindles, 24 weeks pay at 5/- to the workhouse	6	0	0
before he went to ditto, 5 weeks pay at 3/-		15	0
after he come back, 3 weeks at 6/-		18	0
Paid rent to Jno. Watt		8	0
The tailors bill		6	0
An iron pot		2	10
A bed cord		1	2
A cart load of coals and carriage		10	6
Paid for 12 bobbins and two spools		1	5
Given Timothy Barber for his trouble			6
Martha Oliver's child, 52 weeks at 6d.	1	6	0
Sarah Bartington, 52 weeks at 1/-	2	12	0
Mary Yarwood towards coals		7	0
Potatoes and meal		3	0
Barley		2	0
Clothing for John Burgess, his son, coat and shirt		14	0
Clothing for his daughter		5	0
Cash in his illness		3	0
Jno Oak's son, a coat		10	0
James Bason in his wife's illness		10	0
His rent	2	10	0
Spent at town's meeting		2	6

Joseph Legh, senior, 28 weeks at 1/6	2	2	0
ditto , 2 weeks at 2/–		4	0
ditto , 8 weeks at 2/6	1	0	0
ditto , 4 weeks at 3/–		12	0
Given in his illness		8	0
A shirt		2	6
Given by last officer on ditto account		1	0
Paid towards burying ditto	1	1	0
Ditto widow, 10 weeks pay at 1/–		10	0

APPENDIX III

Dorfold MSS, Minute Books

EXTRACTS

Mr. James Hassall of Clotton Hoolfield called with agreements to be signed by Lord Dysart for enclosing the commons and waste lands in Clotton Hoolfield. Says the paper he brought with him to be signed by Lord Dysart was prepared by Mr. Geo. Whitley . . . by the direction of Mr. Arden. 'We whose names are hereunto subscribed being lords of the manor and freeholders of Clotton do agree that the commons and waste lands within the said manor shall be taken in and alloted to us by Commissioners to be hereafter appointed in proportion to our freeholds within the same manor. Witness our hands this fifth day of January, 1805.'

1808, Dec. 24th
Geo. Taylor . . . has a family of 9 children, two of whom are at home and whose wife is dead, applies to take some waste land in Tetton and will bring a character from Mr. Percival. To see Lord Crewe.

1812, Dec. 24th
Joseph Twemlow has a wife and 4 children. The oldest, 18, a soldier in Skipton Mallet, Somersetshire 1st Royals—went 4 years ago a drummer—was with General Moore in Spain. The second, a girl of 16, spins cotton. The 3rd, a son, 13, goes at Christmas to Mr. Sneyd to look after cows. The youngest a girl, 5 years old.

1814, Dec. 24th
James Redfern of Tilsley Bank, near Legh, Lancashire, had a child

about 7 years ago by Sarah Lea. She is dead. Mr. Redfern wishes to take him apprentice as a weaver and thinks the town ought to pay him a fee.

1829, Dec. 29th
Letter to Admiral Tollemache (extracts),

Sir,

We are happy to inform you that notwithstanding the depreciation of agricultural produce your tenants at the rent day . . . paid much better than we expected. By last night's mail we remitted to your bankers, Messrs. Child & Co. £2317. 19. 7 in bills as undermentioned to be placed to your account.

Most of your cheeses are come in and we will very soon send you an account of them as usual and we hope at the same time to send you the conveyance to the trustees of the Birmingham and Liverpool Canal of the land taken from your estate in Edleston for your execution.

Mrs. Ridgeway of Duddon, who is tenant of the enclosure in Clotton, has seen better days. She seems very much inclined to continue your tenant. If you are pleased to consent that she should do so, we will take care that she enters into a proper arrangement for the management of it,

We are Sir,
Your most obliged and
humble servants,
[TOMLINSON & WELSBY]

[On many estates farm produce was taken as part of the rent; in this instance, cheeses].

INDEX OF PERSONS AND PLACES